Delightfully
Southern

Compiled
by
Dot Gibson

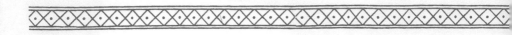

Cover Art: Pamela Gilmore-Hake of Elizabeth, CO

1st printing 10,000
2nd printing 15,000
3rd printing 10,000

Printed in the United States of America
TOOF COOKBOOK DIVISION

670 South Cooper Street
Memphis, TN 38104

TABLE OF CONTENTS

METRIC CONVERSION

U.S.	U.S. Standard Measuring cup 8 ounces	Fluid Ounces	Fluid Metric
1 teaspoon			5ml
3 teaspoons or 1 tablespoon		½	15 ml
2 tablespoons	⅛	1	30 ml
3 tablespoons		1½	45 ml
4 tablespoons	¼	2	60 ml
5⅓ tablespoons	⅓	2½	80 ml
8 tablespoons	½	4	120 ml
12 tablespoons	¾	6	180 ml
16 tablespoons	1 cup	8	240 ml
1 pint	2 cups	16	480 ml
1 quart	4 cups	32	950 ml
1 quart & 3½ tablespoons			1000 ml

APPETIZERS

AND

BEVERAGES

ELEGANT CRAB DIP
Easy and delicious

1 pound crab meat
½ cup margarine
½ cup chopped onion
8 ounces cream cheese

½ teaspoon salt
¼ teaspoon white pepper
¼ teaspoon cayenne pepper
Tabasco to taste

Melt margarine and saute' onions just until limp and transparent. If using a microwave, cook about 3 minutes on high. Add cream cheese and mix well. Add peppers, salt andTabasco. Stir in crab meat. Return to heat just until heated through. Serve with plain crackers or melba toast.

TANGY VEGETABLE DIP

1 cup mayonnaise
2 teaspoons tarragon vinegar
1 teaspoon salt
⅛ teaspoon ground thyme

½ teaspoon curry powder
2 tablespoons chili sauce
1 tablespoon chopped chives
2 tablespoons minced onion

Combine all ingredients; blend well. Refrigerate for several hours or overnight. Serve with raw vegetables.

Yield 1¼ cups

LAYERED TACO-NACHO DIP

1 cup sour cream
½ cup mayonnaise
1 (1¼ ounce) package taco
  seasoning
4 to 6 green onions,
  chopped (tops too)
2 medium tomatoes,chopped

2 (3½ ounce) cans sliced ripe
  olives, drained
2 cups shredded cheddar
  cheese
2 (7 ounce) cans Jalapeno
  bean dip
Lettuce, optional

Combine sour cream, mayonnaise and taco seasoning. Dice entire onion, white and green. Dice tomatoes, drain black olives. Spread bean dip on a large serving plate or tray. Top with layer of sour cream taco mixture, then onions, tomatoes, olives and cheese. If lettuce is desired - finely shred and place around sides.

SHRIMP MOLD

1 (10½ ounce) can cream
  of tomato soup
2 envelopes gelatin
8 ounces cream cheese
½ teaspoon Tabasco
½ teaspoon Worcestershire

½ cup minced onion
1 cup minced celery
1½ cups mayonnaise
2 cups chopped shrimp
salt to taste

Soften gelatin in undiluted soup; heat to dissolve. Add cream cheese, Tabasco, Worcestershire, onion, celery, salt, shrimp and mayonnaise. Mix thoroughly and pour into a fish mold, or casserole dish that has been coated with mayonnaise. Refrigerate. Can be used as appetizer or as salad.

SMOKED SALMON PATE

1 (16 ounce) can salmon
1 (8 ounce) package cream
   cheese
2 tablespoons grated onion
¼ teaspoon salt
1 tablespoon lemon juice
¼ teaspoon Tabasco

1 tablespoon horseradish
1 tablespoon liquid smoke
nuts, finely chopped
parsley
paprika

Drain salmon and remove skin and bones. Combine with cream cheese, onion, salt, lemon juice, Tabasco, horseradish, and liquid smoke; mix well. Place in greased mold or dish. Chill several hours. Remove from mold, place on plate and decorate with nuts, parsley and paprika. Serve with crackers.

CHILI CHEESE BALL

1 (3 ounce) package cream
   cheese
3 cups grated sharp Cheddar
   cheese
2 teaspoons Worcestershire

⅓ teaspoon garlic salt
½ cup finely, chopped nuts
dash of Tabasco
chili powder for garnish

Combine all ingredients and work together with hands until smooth and pliable. Form into 2 balls. Roll in chili powder. Refrigerate until ready to use. Balls may be frozen. Remove from freezer and allow to thaw.

OLIVE BALLS

1 cup grated Cheddar cheese
¼ cup butter or margarine, softened
¼ teaspoon paprika
drop of hot pepper sauce
¾ cup flour
36-40 tiny pimiento-stuffed olives

Combine and mix together cheese, butter, paprika and pepper sauce. Blend in flour. Use a teaspoon of dough per ball. Pat dough into 1½ inch circles. Place olives in center, fold dough around olives and roll in hand to form balls. Place on ungreased cookie sheet and refrigerate 10 minutes. Bake at 375 degrees for 20 minutes. These can be made ahead, and frozen unbaked until needed. When ready to use bake unthawed at 375 degrees for 30 minutes.

MEAT BALLS

2 pounds ground lean chuck
¾ cup crushed flaked corn cereal
1½ teaspoons salt
½ teaspoon pepper
1 (10½ ounce) can onion soup

Sauce:
1 cup chili sauce
1 teaspoon horseradish
1 teaspoon Worcestershire
1 teaspoon Tabasco

Combine meat, cereal crumbs, seasonings, and undiluted soup; mix well. Shape into balls, using one tablespoon of mixture per ball. Bake in an ungreased pan at 400 degrees for 12 to 15 minutes. Combine and heat sauce ingredients. Place meat balls in bowl or chafing dish and pour sauce over top. Serve hot. Meatballs may be made ahead and frozen.

Yield 40 balls

SPINACH BALLS

2 cups herb bread crumbs
2 (10 ounce) boxes frozen
chopped spinach, drained
2 large onions, finely chopped
½ cup Parmesan cheese

6 eggs, beaten
¾ cup margarine
½ teaspoon thyme
1 tablespoon garlic salt
1 tablespoon Accent

Combine all ingredients and mix well. Form into bite-size balls. Place on cookie sheet and bake at 350 degrees for 20 minutes. Serve on warming tray or chafing dish. These balls freeze well. Warm at 350 degrees.

SAUSAGE BALLS

2 cups biscuit mix
1 pound hot sausage

1 cup grated sharp cheese

Combine the 3 ingredients mixing well. Roll into small balls. Bake at 350 degrees for 18 to 20 minutes.

ASPARAGUS ROLL-UP

1 loaf thin sliced bread
1 (15 ounce) can green
   asparagus spears (not
   extra long)
8 ounces cream cheese

6 ounces Roquefort cheese
1 tablespoon mayonnaise
1 egg, beaten
½ cup margarine

Cut crust from bread. Roll each slice with rolling pin. Combine cream cheese, Roquefort and mayonnaise; mix well. Mix in egg. Drain asparagus on paper towels. Spread cheese mixture on bread. Be sure and spread to edges. Place 1 asparagus spear on each slice of bread. Roll bread, jelly-roll style, and press edges to seal. Cut each roll in 3 pieces. Brush with melted margarine. Bake in 350 degree oven until light brown. These can be frozen before baking. Do not bake until ready to serve.

STUFFED MUSHROOMS

1½ pounds large mushrooms
½ cup buttor
1 cup finely chopped onions
¼ bunch parsley, finely
   chopped
2 tablespoons grated
   Swiss cheese

2 tablespoons grated
   Mozzarella cheese
2 tablespoons grated
   Parmesan cheese
Dried bread crumbs

Clean mushrooms and remove stems. Dice stems and enough mushrooms to measure 1½ cups. Melt butter and saute diced mushrooms and onions until soft. Add parsley; remove from heat and cool. Add cheese to mushroom mixture and just enough dry bread crumbs to hold together. Clean out the whole mushrooms, then fill with mixture. Place under broiler until completely heated and browned on top, about 5 minutes. Serve at once.

HOT CHEESE DELIGHTS

1 pound ground beef
1 pound hot pork sausage
1 pound Velveeta cheese
½ teaspoon garlic salt

¼ teaspoon oregano
1 tablespoon Worcestershire
2 loaves party rye or plain
   party bread

Brown beef and sausage in a skillet. Drain off all grease. Cut cheese into small pieces and add to meat. Add garlic salt, oregano, and Worcestershire. Heat and stir until cheese is melted. Spread a rounded teaspoon of cheese mixture on each slice of bread. Bake at 325 degrees for 10 to 12 minutes.

These may be prepared ahead of time and frozen. Spread mixture on bread, place on cookie sheets and freeze. When frozen place in plastic bags until needed. When ready to use place on cookie sheets, allow to thaw and bake as directed.

Yield - 70

CHEESE STRAWS

1 pound Cheddar cheese,
   grated
½ cup margarine or butter,
   softened

1½ cups flour
1 teaspoon salt
¼ teaspoon cayenne pepper

Cream cheese with margarine; add flour, salt and pepper. Place dough in a cookie press and press onto flat pan or cookie sheet. Bake at 350 degrees for 20 minutes.

MINI-QUICHES

½ cup margarine
3 ounces cream cheese
1 cup flour
2 teaspoons minced onion
½ cup grated cheese

2 eggs
½ cup milk
use one: chopped chicken,
   shrimp, or ham
paprika

Combine margarine, cream cheese, and flour; mix well and roll into a ball. Divide into 24 small balls. Place balls in very small muffin tins; press to sides and bottom. Put onion, choice of meat, and cheese in each cup. (Can be frozen or refrigerated at this point). 30 minutes before serving - beat egg and milk together. Fill cups and sprinkle tops with paprika. Bake 10 minutes at 450 degrees. Reduce oven to 350 degrees and bake an additional 10 minutes or until tops brown. Serve at once.

STUFFED CHERRY TOMATO HORS D'OEUVRES

30 cherry tomatoes
¾ cup grated Swiss cheese,
   divided
½ cup finely chopped
   stuffed olives

1 (4½ ounce) can deviled ham
1 tablespoon minced onion

Rinse and dry tomatoes. Cut thin slice off tops and scoop out pulp. Invert on paper towel to drain. Combine ½ cup of the cheese, olives, deviled ham, and onion. Spoon into tomato shells; sprinkle with remaining cheese. Cover and refrigerate until ready to serve.

Yield: 30 servings

CHICKEN LIVER DELIGHTS

12 chicken livers
½ cup soy sauce
12 water chestnuts, halved

brown sugar
12 slices bacon, cut in half

Cut chicken livers in half; soak in soy sauce 4 hours. Drain and slit. Insert half a water chestnut in each. Roll in brown sugar. Wrap livers in half slice of bacon and fasten with toothpick. Dip again in brown sugar. Bake at 400 degrees for 20 to 30 minutes. Turn 2 or 3 times. Keep in warm oven.

PICKLED SHRIMP

5 pounds shrimp -
  boiled, and peeled
2 large onions, sliced
1 (3 ounce) bottle capers &
  liquid
1 teaspoon powdered sugar

1 teaspoon mustard
Dash paprika
2 cups vinegar
2 tablespoons lemon juice
Dash cayenne

Layer shrimp and onions in a deep flat dish or large mouth gift jars. Combine remaining ingredients and pour over shrimp and onions. Cover, place in refrigerator 24 hours before serving. Stir several times.

NUTS AND BOLTS

½ cup margarine
1 teaspoon celery salt
1 teaspoon onion salt
1 teaspoon garlic salt
1½ tablespoons
  Worcestershire sauce

1 tablespoon Tabasco
2½ cups Wheat Chex
2½ cups thin, stick pretzels
2½ cups Rice Chex
1 cup peanuts

Melt margarine in large shallow pan. Stir in celery, onion and garlic salts, Worcestershire and Tabasco. Add cereals, pretzels and nuts. Mix until well coated. Bake in 250 degree oven for 1 hour. Stir every 15 minutes. Spread on paper to cool. Store in tightly covered containers.

CHEESE CUT OUTS

1 cup butter or margarine
1 (1.5 ounce) envelope dry
  onion soup mix

½ pound cheddar cheese,
  grated
2 cups flour

Mix butter and cheese. Add dry soup mix and flour; blend well. Shape into a ball and chill. Roll cheese dough out on a floured surface; cut into desired shapes. If dough is difficult to roll, add a little more flour. Place on a greased cookie sheet and bake at 375 degrees for 10 minutes.

BANANA PUNCH

6 ripe bananas
1 (6 ounce) can frozen
  lemonade concentrate
1 (12 ounce) can frozen
  orange juice concentrate
3 cups warm water

2 cups sugar
1 (46 ounce) can pineapple
  juice
3 (2 liter) bottles lemon-lime
  soda

Thaw frozen concentrates. Place bananas, lemonade and orange juice in blender; blend until smooth. Because of size of recipe remaining ingredients are added in 2 batches. Remove half of mixture from blender and set aside. To remaining mixture add ½ of sugar and ½ of water; blend until smooth. Place in a large freezer container. Place the other half of banana mixture, sugar and water in blender, blend until smooth. Combine with first half in freezer container. Cover and freeze until solid. One hour before serving time remove from freezer. A few minutes before serving place in a large punch bowl. Add pineapple juice and soda. Stir until well blended.

ORANGE BLUSH PUNCH

2 (6 ounce) cans frozen
   orange juice, thawed
2 cups cranberry juice

½ cup sugar
1 quart club soda
ice ring with orange slices

Combine thawed orange concentrate, cranberry juice and sugar; mix well. Chill. When ready to serve, pour in punch bowl and add soda. Freeze water with orange slices and mint leaves in ring mold. Float ice ring in punch bowl.

GOLDEN COOLER

1¼ cups water
¾ cup sugar
3 cups orange juice

3 cups pineapple juice
¾ cup lemon juice
1 (1 liter) bottle ginger ale

Bring water to a boil and add sugar; stir until dissolved. Add fruit juices and mix well. Pour into a gallon milk carton or large freezer container; freeze. Remove from freezer several hours before serving time to allow the mixture to thaw to a slushy stage. Add gingerale, stir and serve. Makes 3 quarts.

VERY GOOD PUNCH

1 (3½ ounce) package
  lime gelatin
1 (3½ ounce) package
  lemon gelatin
2 cups water

2 cups sugar
1 (46 ounce) can pineapple
  juice
2 lemons
32 ounce gingerale

Dissolve flavored gelatin in 2 cups boiling water. Add sugar and stir to dissolve. Add pineapple juice, juice of 2 lemons and enough water to make 1 gallon. Just before serving add 1quart of gingerale.

HOLIDAY MULL

1 (48 ounce) bottle Cranberry
  juice
2 (32 ounce) bottles apple
  juice

½ cup brown sugar
½ teaspoon salt
4 cinnamon sticks
1½ teaspoons whole cloves

Combine cranberry juice, apple juice, brown sugar and salt in electric slow cooker or large sauce pan. Stir until sugar is dissolved. Tie cinnamon sticks and cloves in cheese cloth and place in liquid. Cover pot and cook for 2 hours on low. Do not boil. Electric slow-cooker or crockpot works great. Remove spices and serve.

Yield: 28 (4 ounce) servings

CHRISTMAS EGGNOG

6 eggs, separated
1½ cups sugar, divided
¼ teaspoon salt
6 cups milk

2 cups whipping cream
2 teaspoons vanilla
Ground nutmeg

Beat egg yolks. Gradually add 1 cup of the sugar and the salt beating constantly. Gradually add milk and cream. Cook in a double boiler over hot water. Stir constantly until mixture thickens and coats the spoon. Cool and add vanilla; chill. When ready to serve beat egg whites until foamy. Gradually beat in remaining ½ cup sugar; fold into chilled custard. Spoon into chilled punch bowl and sprinkle with nutmeg.

Yield: 16 servings

TANGY TOMATO COCKTAIL

1 gallon tomato juice
2 teaspoons celery salt
4 teaspoons salt
1 teaspoon onion salt

½ teaspoon Tabasco
½ teaspoon Worcestershire
½ cup sugar

Combine all the ingredients and bring to a boil. Remove from heat; chill.

Yield: 4 quarts

SPICED TEA

1 cup instant tea with lemon
2½ cups orange Tang
2 cups sugar

2 teaspoons cinnamon
1 teaspoon cloves

Combine all ingredients and store in airtight tin or jar. To serve: add 2 teaspoons of mix to a cup of hot water.

HOT CHOCOLATE MIX

2 pound box instant
  chocolate mix
8 quart box powdered milk

8 to 11 ounce jar
  powdered coffee creamer
1 pound box powdered sugar

Mix all ingredients together. Store in airtight container. Mix 4 teaspoons or more to cup of boiling water. This is a large recipe but can be halved.

BREADS

BASIC BISCUITS

Biscuits are the most versatile of all the quick breads. Simple and easy yet delicious and mouth-watering - Southern Biscuits a family favorite.

2 cups all-purpose flour   ¼ cup shortening
1 teaspoon salt   ¾ cup milk
1 tablespoon baking powder

Sift dry ingredients together in a large bowl. Cut in shortening with a pastry blender. Add milk slowly and stir only enough to form a soft dough. Turn the dough onto a floured surface. Knead gently by folding and rolling with hands to get a smooth ball of dough that is not sticky. Roll dough with a floured rolling pin to ½-inch thickness. Dip biscuit cutter into flour, then cut dough. For crusty sides, place biscuits on ungreased baking sheet 1-inch apart for air circulation. For biscuits with soft sides, place them close together in a round 9-inch cake pan. Bake at 450 degrees for 8 to 10 minutes. Serve hot with butter.

Yield: 10 biscuits

ANGEL BISCUITS

These biscuits do have yeast in them but are mixed like a quick bread. This is a large recipe and makes enough for company.

2 packages dry yeast	1 teaspoon salt
¼ cup warm water	3 teaspoons baking powder
5 cups all-purpose flour	1 cup shortening
¼ cup sugar	2 cups buttermilk
1 teaspoon baking soda	⅓ cup margarine, melted

Dissolve yeast in warm water. Sift dry ingredients, and cut in shortening with a pastry blender or food processor. Add the dissolved yeast and buttermilk; stir to make a soft dough. Turn onto a floured surface and knead lightly. Roll out to ½-inch thickness and cut with a floured cutter. Dip biscuits in melted margarine then place on a cookie sheet. Let rise 45 minutes and bake at 375 degrees for 15 minutes or until browned. Serve hot with butter. These may be frozen after they are cut. To bake, allow dough to thaw, let rise 45 minutes, and bake as directed.

Yield: 25 biscuits

BUTTERMILK BISCUITS

2 cups all-purpose flour
1 teaspoon salt
1 tablespoon baking powder

¼ teaspoon baking soda
¼ cup shortening
¾ cup buttermilk

Sift or stir dry ingredients together in a large bowl. Cut in shortening with a pastry blender. Add buttermilk slowly and stir only enough to form a soft dough. Turn the dough onto a floured surface, and knead gently by folding and rolling with hands to get a smooth ball of dough that is not sticky. Roll the dough with a floured rolling pin to ½ inch thickness. Dip a biscuit cutter into flour then cut dough. Place biscuits in a 9-inch round ungreased pan. Bake at 450 degrees for 8 to 10 minutes. Serve hot with butter.

SOUR CREAM BISCUITS

Follow directions for Buttermilk Biscuits. Omit the baking soda and substitute 1 cup sour cream and 2 tablespoons milk for the buttermilk.

HINT - Buttermilk can be made by adding 1 teaspoon of vinegar or lemon juice to 1 cup of milk. Let stand 5 minutes.

CORNBREAD

1 cup corn meal
½ cup sifted plain flour
1 teaspoon salt
¾ teaspoon soda
2 tablespoons sugar

1 egg, well beaten
1½ cups sour milk or
   buttermilk
2 tablespoons vegetable oil

Combine corn meal, flour, salt, soda, and sugar. Mix egg, buttermilk, and oil together; add to dry mixture. Blend well. Pour into a greased and preheated 8x8-inch pan. Bake at 425 degrees for 30 minutes or until done.

Serves 8 to 10

DOUBLE CORNBREAD

1 cup cornmeal
½ teaspoon salt
2 teaspoons baking powder
1 tablespoon sugar

½ cup vegetable oil
2 eggs, slightly beaten
1 cup creamed corn
1 cup sour cream

Combine cornmeal, salt, baking powder and sugar; stir well. Add remaining ingredients; mix well. Pour into a greased, preheated pan or muffin tins. Bake at 400 degrees for 25 to 30 minutes or until browned.

Serves 6 to 8

BREADS

CRACKLIN CORNBREAD

1½ cups corn meal
1 teaspoon salt
1 teaspoon baking powder

1 cup cracklins
1 egg
1½ cups milk or buttermilk

Remove all skin from cracklin. Mix corn meal, salt, and baking powder. Add cracklin. Beat egg and milk and add to dry mixture. Grease heavy skillet and heat. Pour batter in and bake at 450 degrees for 20 minutes.

CUMBERLAND HUSHPUPPIES

2 cups corn meal
2 rounded tablespoons flour
2 rounded teaspoons of
    baking powder
2 rounded teaspoons sugar

1 rounded teaspoon salt
1 small onion, finely chopped
1 cup cream corn
2 eggs
milk

Combine cornmeal, flour, baking powder, sugar, and salt; mix well. Add onion, eggs, corn, and milk. Add just enough milk to make batter consistency to drop from spoon. Drop by tablespoonfuls into hot oil (350 degrees) and cook until golden brown and crisp on outside. Do not put too many in oil at once, will cause oil to cool. Fry both sides, remove and drain on absorbent paper; serve hot.

Yield: 2 dozen puppies

BLUEBERRY MUFFINS

2 eggs, beaten
½ cup sugar
⅓ cup shortening
½ teaspoon salt
2½ cups flour

5 teaspoons baking powder
1 cup milk
1 cup blueberries fresh or
   frozen

Blend eggs, sugar, shortening and salt. Sift flour and baking powder together. Add flour alternately with milk to egg mixture. Add blueberries last. Bake in well greased muffin tins at 350 degrees 20 to 25 minutes.

REFRIGERATOR BRAN MUFFINS

1 cup shortening
2½ cups sugar
4 eggs
1 quart buttermilk
1 pound box Nabisco 100%
   Bran

5 cups flour
5 teaspoons baking soda
1 teaspoon salt
2 cups lukewarm water
1 box seedless raisins

Cream shortening and sugar. Add eggs, beating well. Stir in buttermilk. Add ½ box of Bran. Stir in raisins, flour, baking soda, salt, lukewarm water and remaining Bran cereal. Mix thoroughly; once mixed never stir again. Place in covered container and refrigerate. Will keep 6 weeks in refrigerator. Use as needed. Spoon batter into lightly greased muffin tin and bake at 350 degrees approximately 20 minutes. This mixture makes 5½ quarts.

BREADS

CARROT-POPPY SEED MUFFINS

½ cup flour
½ cup whole-wheat flour
¼ cup brown sugar
1½ teaspoons baking
  powder
¼ teaspoon salt

1 egg, beaten
½ cup milk
2 tablespoons butter or
  margarine, melted
⅓ cup shredded carrots
3 tablespoons poppy seeds

Combine flours, sugar, baking powder and salt; stir to mix well. Combine in a separate bowl egg, milk, and melted margarine; add to the dry ingredients. Stir until moist and lumpy batter forms. Stir in carrots and poppy seeds. Spoon batter into greased muffin tins. Bake in a 375 degree oven 20 to 25 minutes or until a pick inserted into the center comes out clean.

BLUEBERRY LEMON MUFFINS

1 cup blueberries
1 teaspoon grated lemon rind
½ cup plus 2 tablespoons
  sugar
1¾ cups flour
2½ teaspoons baking
  powder

¾ teaspoon salt
1 egg, lightly beaten
¾ cup milk
⅓ cup vegetable oil

Mix blueberries, lemon rind and 2 tablespoons of the sugar; set aside. Combine flour, ½ cup sugar, baking powder and salt. Combine egg, milk and oil; beat with fork. Stir in flour mixture; mix just enough to moisten. There will be lumps. Gently fold in blueberry mixture. Fill greased muffin tins ⅔ full. Bake at 400 degrees for 25 minutes.

BANANA MUFFINS

½ cup margarine
1 cup sugar
2 eggs
2 cups flour
1 teaspoon baking soda

⅛ teaspoon salt
½ cup chopped pecans
3 ripe bananas
1 teaspoon vanilla

Cream margarine and sugar. Add eggs one at a time, beating after each. Combine flour, soda, and salt. Add dry ingredients to creamed mixture. Stir in well mashed bananas, vanilla, and nuts. Spoon into well greased muffin tins. Bake at 325 degrees for 12 to 15 minutes, for small tins and 15 to 20 for regular-size muffins.

DILLY CASSEROLE BREAD

1 package dry yeast
¼ cup warm water
1 cup creamed cottage
   cheese
2 tablespoons sugar
1 tablespoon instant minced
   or 1 medium onion,
   chopped

1 tablespoon margarine,
   melted
2 teaspoons dill seed
1 teaspoon salt
¼ teaspoon baking soda
1 egg
2¼ to 2½ cups flour

Soften yeast in warm water. Heat cottage cheese until warm; add sugar, onion, margarine, dill seed, salt, soda, egg and soften yeast. Add flour in several parts, beating well after each addition. Beat until stiff dough is formed. Cover and let rise in a warm place until light and doubled in size - 50 to 60 minutes. Stir down and turn into well-greased 1½ to 2 quart round casserole. Let rise in warm place for 30 to 40 minutes until doubled in size. Bake at 350 degrees until golden brown, 40 to 50 minutes. Brush top with soft butter and sprinkle with salt. Allow to cool in dish for 5 minutes.

BREADS

BOARDING HOUSE ROLLS

1 package yeast
1½ cups lukewarm water
2 eggs (unbeaten)
4 tablespoons sugar

1 teaspoon salt
¾ cup wesson oil
4½ cups plain flour

Dissolve yeast in lukewarm water. Add other ingredients, adding flour last. Make a soft dough. Knead lightly - set aside in a warm place and let rise until double in bulk. Punch dough down and let rise a second time. Roll out on a floured surface, cut with roll cutter (or biscuit cutter). Dip roll in melted butter and fold over. Let rise again 30 to 35 minutes. Bake at 400 degrees for 10 minutes or until lightly browned.

QUICK ROLLS

2 cups self-rising flour
¼ cup mayonnaise

1 to 1½ cups milk

Mix all ingredients together until smooth. Be sure to use mayonnaise - do not substitute. Divide into 12 rolls and place in greased muffin tins. Bake 400 degrees for 15 minutes.

BEER ROLLS

4 cups commercial
   biscuit mix

1 cup beer
½ cup sugar

Combine biscuit mix and sugar. Add beer and mix. Spoon into greased muffin tins. Bake at 400 degrees for 15 to 20 minutes.

BUTTERSCOTCH COFFEE CAKE

1 (25 ounce) bag frozen
   rolls
¼ cup granulated sugar
1 cup brown sugar

1 (3½ ounce) package butterscotch pudding & pie mix
1 teaspoon cinnamon
½ cup margarine, melted

Cut frozen rolls in half and place in a well-greased tube pan. Combine sugars, cinnamon, and pudding mix (not instant mix). Sprinkle over rolls. Pour margarine over top. Leave out, uncovered, overnight. Rolls will thaw, rise, and be ready to bake by morning. Bake at 350 degrees for 30 minutes. Allow to stand in pan 5 to 10 minutes.

STRAWBERRY NUT BREAD
Pretty and delicious

4 eggs
2 cups sugar
1 cup cooking oil
2 (10 ounce) packages
   frozen strawberries

3 cups flour
1 teaspoon cinnamon
1 teaspoon baking soda
1 teaspoon salt
1 cup chopped nuts

Beat eggs until fluffy; add sugar, oil and thawed strawberries. Combine flour, cinnamon, soda, and salt; sift together. Add to egg mixture and mix well. Stir in nuts. Pour into 2 greased and floured loaf pans. Bake at 350 degrees for 1 hour 10 minutes.

For that little extra, serve with strawberry butter. Mix 2 sticks margarine with ½ cup strawberry jam; blend.

BANANA NUT BREAD

1 cup sugar
1 stick margarine
2 eggs
1½ cups flour

1 teaspoon soda
2 large or 3 small bananas
1 teaspoon vanilla
1 cup chopped nuts

Cream sugar and margarine. Add eggs one at a time. Combine flour and soda; add to mixture. Add mashed bananas, vanilla and nuts. Pour into greased and floured loaf pan. Bake at 350 degrees for 40 to 50 minutes.

CARROT BREAD

1 cup vegetable oil	2 cups sugar
4 eggs	4 teaspoons baking powder
2 teaspoons vanilla	½ teaspoon soda
2 cups grated carrots	½ teaspoon salt
3 cups flour	2 cups chopped pecans

Beat eggs, add oil, vanilla and carrots. Combine flour, sugar, baking powder, soda, salt and nuts. Add to egg mixture and blend well. Pour into 2 greased and floured loaf pans. Bake at 350 degrees for 1 hour to 1 hour and 10 minutes, or until done. Cool in pan for 10 minutes.

GRANOLA

5 cups oatmeal (not quick)	½ cup slivered almonds
1 cup oat bran	½ to ¾ cup vegetable oil
½ cup sesame seeds	¾ to 1 cup honey or cane
½ cup sunflower seeds	syrup
½ cup wheat germ	½ cup raisins

Mix all dry ingredients except for raisins, in a large flat baking pan. Add oil and honey or syrup. Mix well so that all is coated. Bake in a 325 degree oven for 25 to 30 minutes stirring every 10 minutes. Add raisins and bake an additional 5 to 10 minutes. After cereal cooks store in a air tight container. Best kept in refrigerator.

CORNMEAL PANCAKES

1½ cups yellow cornmeal
¼ cup flour
1 teaspoon baking soda
1 teaspoon sugar

1 teaspoon salt
2 cups buttermilk
2 tablespoons oil
1 egg, separated

Combine cornmeal, flour, soda, sugar and salt. In a separate bowl combine and beat buttermilk, oil and egg yolk. Stir into dry ingredients. Beat egg white until stiff peaks form. Fold into batter. Allow to stand 10 minutes. Pour onto greased griddle. When bubbles form on top turn and cook second side.

Yield: 16 to 18 pancakes

MAIN DISHES

BEEF
CHICKEN
PORK
SEAFOOD

COMPANY CASSEROLE

8 ounce package noodles
1 to 1½ pounds ground
  chuck
1 tablespoon margarine
½ cup finely chopped
  green onions

½ cup diced bell pepper
2 (8-ounce) cans tomato
  sauce
1 cup cottage cheese
8 ounces cream cheese
¼ cup sour cream

Cook noodles as directed on package. Drain and set aside.
Brown meat. Saute onions and bell pepper in margarine.
Combine meat, onions, bell peppers and tomato sauce; remove from heat. Combine cottage cheese, cream cheese and
sour cream. Spread half of noodles in a greased 2 quart
casserole. Cover with cheese mixture. Add remaining noodles
and top with meat mixture. Bake uncovered for 35 to 40
minutes at 350 degrees.

Serves 6

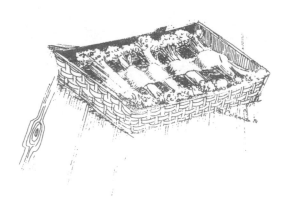

ONE DISH DINNER

1 cup, small macaroni
margarine
1 onion, chopped
1 bell pepper, chopped
1½ to 2 pounds ground beef
1 (8 ounce) can small green
  peas
1 (11½ ounce) can white
  shoepeg corn

1 (10½ ounce) can tomato
  soup
1 (10½ ounce) can mush-
  room soup
1 (8 ounce) can tomato sauce
8 ounces cheddar cheese,
  grated

Cook macaroni according to directions on package; drain.
Saute onions and bell pepper in a small amount of margarine;
set aside. Brown and drain meat. In a large bowl combine
meat, macaroni, onion, bell pepper, peas and corn. Mix tomato soup, mushroom soup, and tomato sauce together. Add
to macaroni mixture, folding in so as not to mash peas. Pour
into 9x13x2 casserole and top with grated cheese. Bake at
350 degrees for 30 minutes.

STUFFED PEPPERS

6 large bell peppers
2 tablespoons oil
1 pound ground beef
½ cup chopped onion
1 (16 ounce) can tomatoes
1 cup water

½ cup regular rice
   (uncooked)
½ teaspoon salt
1 teaspoon Worcestershire
1 cup shredded sharp
   cheese

Slice tops from peppers; remove seeds and membranes. Place in pan, cover with boiling water, and simmer for 5 minutes. Remove from water and drain. Saute onion in vegetable oil, add ground meat and brown. Pour off grease. Add tomatoes, water, rice, salt and Worcestershire sauce. Cover and simmer 30 to 40 minutes or until liquid is absorbed. Remove from heat and add cheese. Stuff peppers with meat mixture. Stand peppers upright in a greased baking dish; add small amount of water. Cover and bake at 350 degrees for 45 minutes. Uncover; bake 15 minutes longer.

MEAT ROLL DELIGHT
Also excellent using Venison

2 eggs, beaten
1 cup soft bread crumbs
⅔ cup tomato sauce
2 tablespoons chopped
   parsley
½ teaspoon oregano
¼ teaspoon salt

¼ teaspoon pepper
¼ teaspoon garlic powder
2 pounds ground beef
8 thin slices of deli ham
1½ cups shredded
   Mozzarella cheese
3 slices Mozzarella cheese

Combine eggs, bread crumbs, tomato sauce, parsley, oregano, salt, pepper, and garlic. Stir in ground meat, mixing well. On waxed paper pat meat into a 12x10 inch rectangle. Arrange ham slices on top of meat, leaving a small margin around edges. Sprinkle shredded cheese over ham. Starting from short end, carefully roll up meat, using paper to lift as you roll. Seal edges and ends. Place roll, seam side down, in a 13x9x2 inch pan. Bake in a 350 degree oven for 55 to 60 minutes, or until done. Remove from oven and place cheese slices over top of roll; return to oven 3 to 5 minutes or until cheese melts. Serves 8 to 10 slices.

PECAN STUFFED MEAT ROLL

1½ pounds ground beef
1½ teaspoons salt
½ teaspoon pepper
2 tablespoons grated onion

¼ cup crumbled fried
  bacon
1 egg, slightly beaten
1 tablespoon milk

Pecan stuffing:
2 cups soft bread crumbs
½ cup chopped pecans
½ cup finely chopped celery
¼ cup milk
2 tablespoons diced,
  green pepper

½ teaspoon salt
¼ teaspoon paprika
¼ cup French salad
  dressing

Combine meat roll ingredients. Mix thoroughly. Press mixture into a rectangle ½ inch thick on waxed paper. Combine all stuffing ingredients except salad dressing. Mix together thoroughly and spoon evenly over meat. Roll up jelly-roll style. Place seam down in greased 8½x4½x2½ loaf pan. Brush top with half of dressing once during baking. Bake in a 350 degree oven for 1 to 1¼ hours. Brush top of loaf with remaining half of French dressing.

Serves 6

QUICK BEEF STROGANOFF

1 pound round steak
½ cup flour
2 tablespoons cooking oil
½ cup chopped onion
1 clove garlic, minced
1 (6-ounce) can mushrooms,
   drained (save juice)

1 cup sour cream
1 (10½ ounce) can cream of
   tomato soup
½ tablespoon Worcestershire
3 drops of Tabasco sauce
½ teaspoon salt
dash of pepper

Cut meat in bite size pieces. Dredge meat in flour, then brown in hot oil. Add onion, garlic and mushrooms. Combine sour cream, tomato soup, mushroom liquid and seasonings. Pour over meat and stir well. Simmer until tender, about 1 hour. Serve over noodles or rice.

Serves 4

VEGETABLE BEEF STEW

2 pounds boneless beef
   chuck steak
flour
3 tablespoons oil
15 pearl onions
1½ cups red wine
½ cup beef broth

4 carrots, sliced
4 stalks celery, diced
1 (10 ounce) package
   frozen green peas
2 tablespoons chopped
   parsley

Cut steak into 3/4 inch cubes. Dredge steak in flour. Heat oil in pan and cook steak in several batches until completely browned. Remove from pan and drain on paper towels. Add onions to pan, cook until lightly browned. Add wine and broth; cook, stirring 1 minute. Return steak to pan. Cover and simmer for 1 hour, stirring occasionally. Add carrots and celery, cover and cook for 20 minutes. Add peas. Cook until steak is tender. When ready to serve sprinkle with parsley.

Serves 4

COTTAGE PIE

3 tablespoons margarine
2 onions, chopped
2 cloves garlic, minced
1 pound ground meat
2 carrots, sliced
¼ cup tomato paste
2 tablespoons chopped
  parsley

1 cup beef broth
1 teaspoon celery salt

TOPPING:
4 large potatoes
3 tablespoons margarine
½ cup finely grated swiss
  cheese

Melt margarine in heavy pan with lid. Add onions, garlic and meat; stir while cooking until meat is browned. Add carrots, tomato paste, parsley flakes, broth and salt. Cover and simmer about 20 minutes or until carrots are tender. Spoon into casserole dish. Spread with potato topping. Bake uncovered at 375 degrees until heated through and browned.

TOPPING: Boil potatoes until tender; drain. Add margarine; mash until smooth. Stir in cheese; mix well.

CROCK POT ROAST

1 roast (4 to 5 pounds)
¼ cup water
1 (10½ ounce) can cream
  of mushroom soup

1 envelope dry onion soup
  mix
1 onion, sliced (optional)

Place water and roast in crock pot. Sprinkle dry soup over meat, add mushroom soup. Add onion slices if more onions are desired. Place lid on pot set on medium and cook 6 to 8 hours. Remove roast to serving platter. Gravy can be thickened if needed.

HEARTY BEEF STEW

2 pounds stew meat
  cut in 1½ inch cubes
¼ cup flour
¼ cup shortening or oil
4¼ cups water, divided
1 (8 ounce) can tomato sauce
¼ cup chopped onions plus
3 medium onions, quartered
½ teaspoon garlic salt
1 bay leaf
2 teaspoons salt
¼ teaspoon pepper
6 medium potatoes,
  peeled and quartered
6 medium carrots,
  cut in 1 inch pieces
¼ cup cornstarch

Biscuits:
2 cups flour
3 teaspoons baking powder
1 teaspoon salt
⅓ cup shortening
¾ cup milk

Dredge meat in flour. Heat oil in a Dutch oven and brown meat. Add 4 cups of the water, tomato sauce, chopped onion, garlic salt, bay leaf, salt and pepper. Bring to a boil, reduce heat, cover, and simmer for 1½ to 2 hours, or until meat is tender. Add potatoes, onions and carrots; cover and simmer until vegetables are tender about ½ hour. Blend cornstarch and ¼ cup water; add to stew and stir until boils. Simmer 5 minutes. Put stew in a large shallow baking dish or pan and top with biscuits. Bake at 425 degrees for 20 to 25 minutes.

Biscuits - Combine flour, baking powder and salt in a bowl. Cut in shortening until mixture resembles coarse meal. Add milk and stir just enough to moisten well. Knead dough 8 to 10 times on lightly floured surface. Roll or pat to ½ inch thickness. Cut into 2 inch biscuits.

COUNTRY FRIED STEAK

6 to 8 cubed steaks
1 teaspoon salt
1 teaspoon pepper
½ cup milk
½ cup flour

oil for frying

Gravy
2 tablespoons flour
1 cup milk

Sprinkle steaks with salt and pepper. Mix flour, remaining salt and pepper together. Dip cubed steaks into milk and dredge in flour mixture. Heat oil in fry pan. Place steaks in hot oil and fry on both sides until browned. For thicker "real country crust" dredge steaks first in flour, dip in milk and then dredge steaks again in flour. Remove steaks, pour off excess oil leaving about 2 tablespoons. Add 2 tablespoons flour; stir and brown over medium heat. Add milk, stirring constantly until thickened. Add water or more milk if thinner gravy is desired.

SLOPPY JOES
Young peoples delight

2 pounds ground beef
1 onion, chopped
½ cup chopped celery
2 tablespoons prepared
  mustard

1 cup water
½ cup catsup
1 (10½ ounce) can cream
  of tomato soup
salt to taste

Place ground meat, onion and celery in a frying pan. Cook over medium to medium high heat until meat is browned. Add remaining ingredients. Simmer until mixture thickens. Spoon into hamburger buns and serve while hot.

CHICKEN PARMESAN

Boned, skinned chicken
   breast halves
Salt
Butter or margarine, melted

Parmesan cheese
Bread crumbs

Sprinkle chicken lightly with salt. In a shallow dish combine Parmesan and crumbs in equal amounts for coating. Dip each piece of chicken in melted margarine and then dredge in cheese-crumb mixture. Make sure pieces are well coated; roll. Place rolled breast, seam down, in a shallow baking dish. Sprinkle a little extra Parmesan over top. Bake at 350 degrees for 45 minutes or until done.

CHICKEN BREASTS IN SOUR CREAM

8 to 10 chicken breast
   halves, skinned and boned
sliced ham or dried chipped
   beef

2 (10½ ounce) cans
   Cream of Mushroom Soup
1 cup sour cream
1 (6 ounce) can mushrooms

Line bottom of a greased casserole with ham or dried chipped beef; place chicken on top. Mix sour cream and mushroom soup. Pour soup mixture over chicken. Bake at 325 degrees for 1½ hours. Add mushrooms the last 15 minutes.

CHICKEN 'N RICE CASSEROLE

5 cups of cooked rice
5 cups cooked chopped
  chicken
2 (10½ ounce) cans
  cream of chicken soup
2 cups mayonnaise
2½ teaspoons minced onion

2½ cups chopped celery
2½ teaspoons lemon juice
5 hard cooked eggs,
  chopped
2½ cups crumbled Corn
  Flakes cereal
1 cup slivered almonds

Mix all ingredients except cereal flakes and almonds. Pour into greased casserole, sprinkle with cereal crumbs and almonds. Bake at 375 degrees for 1 hour.

CHICKEN-BROCCOLI CASSEROLE

4 whole chicken breasts
2 (10 ounce) packages
  frozen broccoli
¼ teaspoon curry powder
1 (10½ ounce) can
  cream of chicken soup

⅔ cup mayonnaise
⅓ cup evaporated milk
½ cup grated American
  cheese
1 cup buttered bread crumbs

Cook chicken breast and remove bones; cut into bite size pieces. Cook broccoli according to directions on package; drain. Place broccoli in bottom of greased casserole. Place chicken pieces on top of broccoli. Mix together curry, soup, mayonnaise, milk and cheese; pour over broccoli and chicken. Top with crumbs. Bake at 350 degrees for 30 minutes.

CHICKEN POTATO BAKE

1 (32 ounce) package frozen
hash brown potatoes
1 teaspoon salt
¼ teaspoon pepper
4 cups diced, cooked chicken
1 (4 ounce) can sliced
mushrooms, drained
1 cup sour cream
2 cups chicken broth

1 (10½ ounce) can cream
of chicken soup
2 teaspoons instant chicken
bouillon granules
2 tablespoons finely chopped
onions
1 clove garlic, minced
Paprika
¼ cup sliced almonds

Thaw potatoes; spread in an ungreased 13x9x2 inch baking dish. Sprinkle with salt and pepper. Place chopped chicken on potatoes; add mushrooms. Combine sour cream, chicken broth, soup, bouillon granules, onions and garlic; mix well and pour over chicken. Sprinkle paprika and almonds over top. Bake in a 350 degree oven, uncovered for 50 to 60 minutes.

Yields 8 to 10 servings

CHICKEN PIE SOUFFLE

8 slices white bread
Butter or margarine
2 cups cooked, diced
  chicken
½ cup diced onions
½ cup diced celery
½ cup diced bell pepper
1 hard-boiled egg, sliced

½ cup mayonnaise
salt and pepper to taste
1½ cups milk
2 eggs, slightly beaten
1 (10 ounce) can cream of
  chicken soup
1 cup grated sharp cheese

Butter bread slices, remove crust and cut in cubes. Place half in bottom of buttered baking dish. Combine chicken, onions, celery, bell pepper, egg, mayonnaise and seasoning. Spread over bread cubes. Place remaining half bread cubes over mixture. Beat eggs and milk together; pour over bread. Cover and refrigerate several hours or over night. When ready to bake spoon soup over casserole. Bake at 350 degrees for 40 minutes. Add cheese and bake an additional 10 minutes.

EASY CRUST CHICKEN PIE

1 2½ - 3 pound fryer
½ cup margarine
¾ cup flour
½ teaspoon baking powder
¼ teaspoon pepper

1 cup milk
1 egg, beaten
2 eggs, hard boiled
1½ cups chicken stock

Cook chicken in salted water until tender. Remove from broth; remove skin and bones and cut chicken into bite size pieces. Simmer stock down to 1½ cups. Melt margarine in a casserole or 9x9 cake pan. Combine flour, baking powder, pepper, milk and 1 egg. Pour this thin batter into dish. Top with chopped chicken and 2 hard cooked eggs, sliced. Pour chicken stock carefully over top. Bake in a 350 degree oven for about 1 hour. The batter will rise and form a brown crusty topping.

Yield: 6

CHICKEN TETRAZZINI

6 to 8 mushrooms
6 tablespoons butter or
  margarine
½ cup sherry
6 tablespoons flour
3 cups hot milk
½ teaspoon salt

¼ teaspoon pepper
1 cup cream
2 egg yolks
5 cups diced chicken
9 ounce package thin
  spaghetti
1 cup Parmesan cheese

Cook spaghetti according to package direction; drain and set aside. Saute mushrooms in 2 tablespoons butter; add sherry. Simmer a few minutes then set aside. Make white sauce with remaining butter, flour, and hot milk. Season with salt and pepper, beat egg yolks into cream. Stir white sauce into egg mixture, then return to sauce pan and cook for 5 minutes, stirring constantly. Remove from heat, add chicken and mushrooms. Place cooked spaghetti in a 9x13x2 inch casserole. Add chicken mixture and top with cheese. Bake at 350 degrees for 20 to 30 minutes or until bubbly.

CHICKEN AND DUMPLINGS

3 pounds of chicken pieces
2 ribs of celery
1 medium onion, quartered
salt and pepper
2 tablespoons flour
¼ cup milk

DUMPLINGS:
2 cups packaged
   biscuit mix
2 cups flour
½ cup milk

Put chicken, celery, and onions in 6 quart pot. Cover with water; add salt and pepper. Cook covered until chicken is tender. Remove chicken from broth; skin, remove bones and cut into chunks. Discard celery and onion. Strain and measure broth. Add water to broth if necessary to have 4 quarts of liquid. Return broth to pot. Make a smooth paste of flour and milk and stir into broth. Dumplings: Mix biscuit mix and flour together. Add about ½ cup milk. Place on floured surface and knead lightly. Roll out and cut in 1½ inch squares. Bring broth to a boil and drop in pieces of dumplings. Cook covered on simmer until dumplings are done (about 20 minutes). Watch closely to keep from sticking. Place chicken pieces on top at end of cooking time to reheat.

SOUTHERN FRIED CHICKEN

chicken pieces
eggs
milk

flour
salt and pepper

Cut chicken into pieces; sprinkle with a little salt. Beat eggs with a little milk (usually 2 eggs and ¼ cup milk). Put flour in bag and add salt and pepper. Dip each piece of chicken in egg mixture, drop in bag and shake to coat with flour. Fry in deep fryer or skillet. Makes beautiful, golden, crisp crust.

BAKED CHICKEN SQUARES WITH MUSHROOM SAUCE

6 cups diced cooked chicken
3 cups soft bread crumbs
1½ cups cooked rice
¾ cup chopped onion
¾ cup chopped celery
⅓ cup chopped pimiento
¾ teaspoon salt
¾ teaspoon poultry seasoning

1½ cups chicken broth
1½ cups milk
4 eggs, lightly beaten
SAUCE
1 (10½ ounce) can
  cream of mushroom soup
¼ cup milk
1 cup sour cream

Combine all ingredients for casserole. Spoon into a 9x13 inch baking dish. Bake at 350 degrees for 50 to 55 minutes or until knife inserted in center comes out clean. Combine mushroom soup, milk and sour cream in a double boiler. Stir until heated. Cut casserole into squares and serve with hot sauce.

Serves 6

ST. PAUL'S RICE CASSEROLE

1 pound pork sausage
4½ cups boiling water
1 package (2 envelopes)
   Lipton's chicken noodle
   soup
½ cup regular rice

1 large bell pepper,
   chopped
1 large onion, chopped
2 ribs celery, chopped
½ cup slivered almonds

Brown sausage; drain on paper towel. Add dry soup mix and rice to boiling water; cook for 7 minutes. Remove from heat. Add drained sausage, bell pepper, onion, celery, and almonds. Pour into a casserole and bake uncovered at 350 degrees for 1 hour.

PORK CHOP & ONION RICE BAKE

6 to 8 pork chops
2 tablespoons margarine
1 cup uncooked regular rice
1 (1 ounce) envelope
   onion soup mix

1 (4 ounce) can sliced
   mushrooms
Hot Water

Melt margarine in fry pan and brown chops. Spread rice in bottom of 13x9x2 baking pan. Sprinkle onion mix over rice. Drain mushrooms, reserving liquid; distribute mushrooms over rice. Add enough hot water to mushroom liquid to equal 3 cups; pour over rice. Place browned chops on top of rice. Cover tightly with foil; bake in a 350 degree oven for 45 minutes to 1 hour, depending on thickness of chops. Remove foil. If any liquid remains continue cooking a few minutes, uncovered until liquid evaporates.

HAM SLICES AND RED EYE GRAVY

Ham slices ¼ inch thick
¼ cup water

¼ cup strong black coffee

Cut slits in fat around ham slices to prevent curling. Brown ham in heavy skillet, turning several times. Cook slowly until ham is browned. Add water and let ham simmer for a few minutes. Remove ham from skillet and add strong coffee to pan drippings. Bring to a boil. Serve with grits.

PORK ROAST WITH APPLES

4 to 5 pounds boneless
   rolled pork loin roast
1 teaspoon ground ginger
½ teaspoon ground nutmeg

½ teaspoon ground cinnamon
1 teaspoon salt

SPICED APPLES
2 medium apples
¼ cup honey
½ cup water
1 tablespoon lemon juice

¼ teaspoon ground ginger
¼ teaspoon ground cinnamon
¼ teaspoon ground nutmeg

Combine ginger, nutmeg, cinnamon and salt. Rub mixture over roast. Place roast on a rack in a baking pan. Insert meat thermometer and bake uncovered at 325 degrees for 2 to 2½ hours or until thermometer reads 160 degrees. Remove from heat, cover and let stand 15 minutes. APPLES - Combine honey, water, lemon juice, ginger, cinnamon and nutmeg in a medium size pan. Bring to a boil. Reduce heat and simmer uncovered until it begins to thicken. Peel, core and slice apples. Add apples to liquid and continue cooking until apples are tender. Stir often, but gently. Serve over pork slices.

PORK TENDERLOIN

2 (1 pound) pork
   tenderloins
2 strips of bacon
½ cup soy sauce
1 tablespoon vinegar

¼ teaspoon pepper
½ teaspoon sugar
2 tablespoons grated onion
1 clove of garlic, minced

Wrap tenderloins in bacon and hold in place with toothpicks. In a small bowl combine, soy sauce, vinegar, pepper, sugar, onion and garlic. Pour sauce over tenderloins and allow to marinate several hours. Turn tenderloins several times. Bake tenderloins uncovered in a 350 degree oven for 1½ hours. Baste occasionally. Add water if needed while cooking.

BREAKFAST CASSEROLE SUPREME

10 slices white bread
1 pound ground sausage
6 eggs
3 cups milk
¾ teaspoon dry mustard

½ teaspoon salt
¼ teaspoon white pepper
2 cups shredded sharp
   cheese
2 cups shredded mild cheese

Remove crust from bread; cut into squares. Fry sausage, drain well. Arrange half of bread squares in bottom of lightly greased 13x8½x2 inch casserole. Top with sharp cheese, then sausage, remaining bread squares and then mild cheese. Dissolve mustard in a little of the milk. Beat eggs, add milk, mustard, salt & pepper. Pour mixture over layers. Cover and refrigerate overnight. Bake uncovered in a 350 degree oven for 1 hour or until firm and browned.

CRAB CAKES

1½ pounds crabmeat
1½ teaspoons salt
1 teaspoon black pepper
1½ teaspoons dry mustard
1½ teaspoons Worcester-
   shire sauce

1 egg yolk
2 teaspoons mayonnaise
1½ teaspoons chopped
   parsley

Mix all ingredients and shape into 6 cakes. Place in frying pan with small amount of margarine. Cook over medium heat, browning on both sides.

CRAB CASSEROLE

½ cup butter or margarine
4 heaping tablespoons flour
2 cups milk
4 teaspoons lemon juice
2 teaspoons prepared
   mustard
2 teaspoons salt

4 hard boiled eggs,
   chopped
½ cup onions
1 cup mayonnaise
1 pound crabmeat
2 cups buttered bread
   crumbs

Melt margarine, stir in flour, and slowly add milk. Stir constantly until white sauce is formed. Add the remaining ingredients except for bread crumbs. Pour into a greased baking dish. Top with bread crumbs. Bake at 350 degrees for 35 to 45 minutes.

BAKED CROQUETTES
(Tuna or Salmon)

2 (6½-ounce) cans tuna,
  chicken, or turkey or
  1 (14-ounce) can salmon
1 cup fresh bread crumbs
½ cup wheat germ
¼ cup chopped onion

½ teaspoon salt
¼ teaspoon pepper
½ cup mayonnaise
2 teaspoons lemon juice
¼ cup evaporated milk
wheat germ for coating

Drain liquid from meat into a medium size bowl. To liquid, add bread crumbs and ½ cup wheat germ. Blend well. Stir in onion, salt, pepper, mayonnaise, lemon juice and milk. Flake meat and add to mixture. Divide mixture into 8 or 10 parts. Shape into croquettes, cones or ovals. Roll lightly in wheat germ. Place on foil lined cookie sheet. Bake 20 minutes at 375 degrees. Serve with catsup or tartar sauce.

SHRIMP AND CHEESE CASSEROLE

1 pound shrimp (boiled,
  and peeled)
6 slices bread
½ pound grated mild cheese
¼ cup butter, melted

3 eggs, beaten
½ teaspooon dry mustard
salt to taste
2 cups milk

Break bread into bite size pieces. Arrange in layers; bread, shrimp, cheese. There should be at least 2 layers of each. Pour butter over top. Beat eggs, mustard and salt together; add milk. Pour over layers. Let stand in refrigerator 3 hours minimum, preferably overnight. Bake covered at 350 degrees for 1 hour.

Serves 4 or 5

SHRIMP PILAU

4 slices bacon
1 cup rice
2 cups shrimp
1 teaspoon Worcestershire
1 tablespoon flour

3 tablespoons butter
  or margarine
½ cup chopped celery
¼ cup chopped bell pepper
salt and pepper

Fry bacon until crisp; set aside. Cook rice according to directions. Sprinkle shrimp with Worcestershire and dredge in flour. Saute celery and bell pepper in butter. Add shrimp, salt and pepper; simmer until flour is cooked. Stir in cooked rice. Add extra butter if needed. Stir in crumbled bacon.

Serves 6

SHRIMP IN GARLIC BUTTER

2 pounds large raw shrimp
½ cup butter or margarine
½ cup olive oil
¼ cup chopped parsley,
  divided

3 cloves garlic, crushed
1 teaspoon salt
dash of cayenne
¼ cup lemon juice

Remove shells, leaving tails on. Rinse under cold water; drain and pat dry. Melt butter in 13x9x2 inch baking dish. Add oil, 2 tablespoons parsley, garlic, salt, cayenne, and lemon juice; mix well. Add shrimp, tossing lightly in mixture to coat well. Arrange in single layer in baking dish. Bake at 400 degrees for 9 to 10 minutes. Using tongs, remove shrimp to heated platter. Pour garlic mixture over shrimp or serve in a pitcher. Sprinkle shrimp with remaining chopped parsley. Garnish platter with lemon slices.

Serves 8

SHRIMP JAMBALAYA

1 pound shrimp, peeled and deveined
1/4 cup margarine or oil
1 cup minced onion
2 cloves garlic, minced
2 green peppers, diced
1 1/2 cups cooked regular rice
1 (20-ounce) can tomatoes, chopped
2 cups water
1 tablespoon salt
1/4 teaspoon pepper
1 bay leaf
1 pound cooked ham, cut into 1/2 inch cubes

Saute shrimp in oil 2 to 3 minutes, or until pink; remove from pan and set aside. Add onion, garlic and green pepper to remaining oil. Cook 2 minutes, stirring occasionally. Stir in rice; mix well. Add tomatoes, water, salt, pepper and bay leaf; bring to a boil. Cover, reduce heat and simmer 15 minutes. Add ham and shrimp; cover and cook 10 minutes or until all liquid is absorbed.

Serves 6 or 8

SHRIMP CREOLE

2 pounds shrimp
6 tablespoons margarine
1 small onion, chopped
1/2 bell pepper, chopped
1 cup chopped celery
1 (15-ounce) can tomato sauce
1 tablespoon sugar
1/4 teaspoon pepper

Boil shrimp; peel and devein. Saute onions, pepper, and celery in margarine. Add tomato sauce, sugar, pepper, and shrimp. Cook 10 minutes. Serve over rice.

FRIED SHRIMP BATTER

Shrimp
1 cup flour
1 egg
2 tablespoons vegetable oil

1 cup ice water
1 teaspoon salt
1 teaspoon sugar

Peel shrimp, leaving tails on. Mix all ingredients together. Dip shrimp into batter then drop into hot oil. Batter is best if kept chilled while frying shrimp.

COASTAL SEAFOOD CASSEROLE

1 cup crab meat
1 cup boiled and peeled
   shrimp
1 cup chopped green peppers
1 cup chopped onion
1 cup chopped celery
¼ teaspoon salt

1 teaspoon pepper
1 teaspoon Worcestershire
1 cup mayonnaise
1 (8 ounce) can water
   chestnuts, chopped
buttered bread crumbs

Mix together all ingredients except buttered bread crumbs. Place in a greased casserole, and sprinkle top with crumbs. Bake 30 minutes at 350 degrees.

POACHED ATLANTIC SALMON

6 (8 ounce) salmon fillets
2 tablespoons butter or
  margarine
2 tablespoons flour
1 cup milk, heated
salt and pepper

2 eggs, hard boiled
4 cups water
3 bay leaves
1 tablespoon vinegar
½ cup dry white wine

Make a white cream sauce by melting butter over low heat, slowly stirring in flour and cooking until well blended. Add warm milk slowly, stirring constantly, and cook until the sauce is thick and smooth. Add salt and pepper to taste. Chop eggs and add. Combine water, bay leaves, vinegar and a pinch of salt in a fish poacher or large pot. Place over medium heat. When simmering add wine and fillets. Continue to simmer about 10 minutes for each inch of thickness. (Measured at thickest part of filet) Fish should be firm to the touch but not over cooked. Remove fillets from liquid and drain. Place on dinner plates and spoon warm sauce over fillets.

STUFFED SOLE

4 fillets of sole,
  4 ounces each
1 medium onion, diced
1 cup celery, finely diced
4 tablespoons butter or
  margarine
2 cups white bread, cubed

1½ cups cracker crumbs
1 pound crab meat
1 teaspoon Worcestershire
  sauce
mayonnaise
salt and pepper

Combine bread, cracker crumbs and crab meat in a mixing bowl. Saute onions and celery in 2 tablespoons of the butter; add to crab. Add Worcestershire sauce and enough mayonnaise to enable the mixture to hold together well. Salt and pepper to taste. Place ¼ cup of stuffing on each fillet. Any extra stuffing place around fish. Brush or drizzle remaining butter over fillets. Bake uncovered in a 350 degree oven for 20 to 25 minutes or until fish is flaky. (Fillet can be rolled after stuffing to form fish rolls. Place seam down and bake the same).

BAKED FISH FILLETS I
(Groupers, Snapper, Bass)

boned, skinned fillets (thick)
salt and pepper
butter

diced onion
1 (12-ounce) can evaporated
  milk

Use thick fillets of any fish. Salt and pepper. Completely fill a greased baking dish with fillets. Place pieces close together. It is necessary to fill the entire dish. Place pat of butter on each fillet. Cover with diced onions. Pour enough evaporated milk into baking dish to come to top of onions, but not enough to float them. Bake at 350 degrees for 1½ hours, or until golden brown and moisture is baked out. Baste occasionally. Delicious.

BAKED FISH FILLETS II

2 to 3 pounds fish	dry white wine
¼ pound butter	salt, pepper, paprika
lemon juice	Parmesan cheese

Use fillet of any fish. Salt and pepper fillets. Put butter in shallow baking dish in hot oven (400 to 500 degrees) until it is browned. (This adds to flavor). Place fillets flesh side down in sizzling butter. Bake 10 to 15 minutes. Turn carefully with spatula; baste. Sprinkle each fillet with lemon juice, wine, Parmesan cheese and paprika. Bake 5 more minutes or until done. Run under broiler if more brownness is desired. Baste with sauce and serve.

LOW COUNTRY BROILED FISH

fillets of fish	lemon juice
mayonnaise	white wine
lemon pepper	paprika

This is great for red fish, sea trout, whiting, blues, or flounder. Spread fillets with mayonnaise (spread as if you are buttering toast). Sprinkle lemon pepper, lemon juice and white wine over entire surface. Sprinkle with a little paprika for garnish. Broil until done (time depends on thickness of fillets).

FISH SQUARES

2 pounds white meat fish (snapper, flounder, grouper,) or 2 packages frozen perch, halibut or white meat fish
3 eggs, lightly beaten
1 cup milk
1 cup saltine cracker crumbs

1 tablespoon chopped parsley
1 tablespoon minced onion
Juice of 1 lemon
salt and pepper
½ cup butter or margarine

Salt fish and bake. Remove bones and shred meat. Place in bowl and add eggs; mix well. Add milk, parsley, onion, lemon juice, salt, pepper and half of the cracker crumbs and melted butter. Place in baking dish and top with remaining cracker crumbs and melted butter. If mixture seems too dry add a little more milk. Set casserole in pan of hot water. Bake at 325 degrees for 50 minutes. Serve with tartar sauce.

ESCALLOPED OYSTERS

½ cup cracker crumbs
   (saltines coarsely crumbled)
¼ cup bread crumbs
¼ cup butter, melted
salt

1 cup oysters and some
   liquor (18 to 20 oysters)
Dash of Tabasco
1 tablespoon light cream

Combine cracker crumbs, bread crumbs and butter; stir until well mixed. Spread half of the crumb mixture in bottom of a shallow baking dish. Place oysters on top of crumbs; add a little of liquor and a pinch of salt. Combine cream and Tabasco sauce; drizzle over oysters. Cover with remaining crumbs. Bake at 400 degrees for about 20 minutes or until crumbs are browned and edges are bubbling.

FRIED OYSTERS

2 dozen oysters
2 eggs
2 tablespoons milk

salt and pepper
1 cup corn meal or
crumbs

Rinse oysters. Beat eggs, milk, and seasoning together. Dip oysters in beaten egg mixture and roll in meal or crumbs. Fry in deep fat at 375 degrees about 2 minutes or in frying pan a couple minutes on each side.

SOUPS

AND

SALADS

GEORGIA BRUNSWICK STEW

3 to 4 pounds chicken
Salt
1 to 1½ pounds ground or
    chopped beef or venison
2 to 3 onions, chopped
1 (15 ounce) can yellow corn
2 (15 ounce) cans green peas
2 (15 ounce) cans lima beans

1 (15 ounce) can cream corn
1 (16 ounce) can tomatoes,
    chopped
1 cup catsup
1 cup barbecue sauce
3 tablespoons Worcestershire
Salt and pepper

Place chicken in soup kettle with enough water to cover; add salt. Cook 1½ hours or until tender. Remove chicken from broth; bone chicken, cut into small pieces and return to broth. Brown ground meat in small amount of oil. Add onion and cook until tender but not browned; add to broth. Drain corn, peas and lima beans; add to soup. Add creamed corn, chopped tomatoes, catsup, barbecue sauce and Worcestershire sauce. Salt and pepper to taste. Cover and simmer for 2½ to 3 hours. Stir often.

COLONIAL CHEDDAR SOUP

⅓ cup shredded carrots
2 tablespoons minced onion
¼ cup butter or margarine
a cup flour
dash of pepper

½ teaspoon salt
4 cups milk
2 cups shredded Cheddar
    cheese

Sauté onion and carrots in butter. Stir in flour, salt and pepper. Gradually add milk, stir until thickened. Add cheese; stir until melted. Serve with crackers.

COUNTRY SAUSAGE SOUP

A very thick soup. Excellent for a wintery night supper.

1½ pounds smoked
  large link sausage
3 (16 ounce) cans chopped
  tomatoes
2 medium onions, finely
  chopped

9 cups water, divided
4 average potatoes, chopped
1¾ cups rice, (not instant)
salt

Cut sausage into ¼ inch slices, then cut slices in half. In a large heavy pan or dutch oven bring tomatoes and 2 cups water to a boil; add sausage, cover and cook 30 minutes. Dip grease off top and discard. While sausage is cooking, cut potatoes into very small cubes, about ½ to ¾ inches. Add remaining water to tomatoes and return to boil. Add onions and potatoes; reduce heat, cover and simmer 30 minutes. Add rice, cover and continue to cook for 30 minutes or until rice is tender. Caution - once rice is added you must stir often to prevent sticking. This is a thick soup. You do not want it watery. Add salt if needed.

CREAM OF CORN SOUP

½ cup butter or margarine
1 large onion, chopped
4 large stalks celery, chopped
¼ cup chopped green pepper
4 tablespoons flour

1 quart milk
2 (16 ounce) cans cream
  style corn
2 tablespoons sugar
salt and pepper

Melt butter in a 3 quart saucepan. Saute onions, celery, and green peppers. When vegetables are soft, stir in flour. Slowly add a little milk, stirring to form a cream sauce. Add corn, remaining milk, and sugar. Season to taste. Heat until serving temperature.

SENATE NAVY BEAN SOUP

1½ cups navy beans
1¾ pounds smoked ham
   hocks
1 cup finely chopped onion
2 tablespoons margarine
1 cup finely chopped celery
1 small clove garlic, mashed

2 cups finely chopped
   potatoes
1 bay leaf
salt to taste (depends on
   ham hock)
1 tablespoon chopped parsley

Soak navy beans in 1 quart of water for 3 to 4 hours. Place
ham hocks in 3 quarts of water; bring to a boil, lower heat
and simmer for at least 2 hours. In a large soup pot, saute
onions in margarine; add celery and mashed garlic. Add
potatoes and 2 cups of water from the ham hocks. Cover
and cook 15 to 20 minutes. Add beans and liquid, ham hocks
with remaining liquid, and bay leaf. Cover and cook slowly
until beans are tender, about 1 hour. Add water if needed.
Remove ham hocks, cut meat from bones into bite size pieces
and return to soup. Salt to taste. (This will depend on the
ham hock). Sprinkle with parsley and serve.

Serves 4 to 6

DOWN HOME CHILI

2 pounds ground meat
2 to 3 medium onions, chopped
1 bell pepper, chopped
2 bay leaves
½ teaspoon oregano
1 (12 ounce) can tomato paste
4 cups water

1 tablespoon salt
Pepper to taste
2 to 3 tablespoons chili powder
1 to 2 cloves garlic, minced
¼ teaspoon cumin
2 (15 ounce) cans pinto or kidney beans

Brown meat in large, heavy pot, 5 quart size. Add onion, bell pepper and cook until limp. Add remaining ingredients except for beans. Simmer for 1½ hours. Add pinto or kidney beans and simmer for 30 minutes.

BLACK BEAN SOUP

1 (8 ounce) package black beans
¼ cup margarine
1 small onion, chopped
1 cup diced celery
1 clove garlic

2 quarts water
2 teaspoons salt
1 teaspoon pepper
¼ teaspoon dry mustard
dash cayenne pepper or Tabasco sauce

Wash beans and soak overnight; drain. Sauté onions, celery, and garlic in margarine. Combine beans, water, and sauted onions and celery; add salt, pepper, mustard and hot seasoning. Cover and cook over low heat until beans are tender. Remove 1 cup of beans, mash and return to pot. This can be served over rice accompanied with chopped onions or as soup.

WILLIAMSBURG PEANUT SOUP

¼ cup margarine or butter
1 medium onion, chopped
2 ribs celery, chopped
3 tablespoons all purpose
  flour

2 quarts chicken stock or
  canned chicken broth
2 cups smooth peanut butter
1¾ cup light cream
chopped peanuts for garnish

Sauté onion and celery in butter until soft, but not brown.
Stir in flour until well blended. Add chicken stock, stirring
constantly, and bring to a boil. Remove from heat and rub
through sieve. Add peanut butter and cream, stirring to blend
thoroughly. Return to low heat, but do not boil. Serve gar-
nished with peanuts.

ONION SOUP

5 cups thinly sliced onions
¼ cup butter or margarine
¼ teaspoon pepper
½ teaspoon salt
¼ teaspoon sugar
3 tablespoons flour
3 cups boiling water
2 (10½ ounce) cans
  beef broth

1 (10½ ounce) can chicken
  broth
½ cup dry white wine
  (optional)
8 slices french bread,
  toasted
8 slices Mozzarella cheese
½ cup grated Parmesan

Melt margarine in a dutch oven. Saute' onions over medium
heat; do not brown. They should be a golden shade. While
onions cook (about 15 minutes) sprinkle with pepper, salt,
and sugar. Sprinkle flour on onions; stir. Add hot water
and broth. Stir in wine. Cover dutch oven and simmer gently
for 20 minutes. While soup is simmering toast bread. Place
toast in each oven proof serving bowl. Ladle soup over bread,
top with slice of Mozzarella and sprinkle Parmesan over top.
Place in oven on broil, about 6 inches from heat, until cheese
melts.

8 servings

FISH CHOWDER

4 to 5 pounds fish (any
   white flaky meat fish)
4 cups diced potatoes
3 cups chopped onions
1 cup chopped celery
4 cups liquid including stock

1 quart milk
1 stick butter or margarine
salt to taste
½ teaspoon pepper
½ teaspoon Accent
2 teaspoons Italian seasoning

Use any baking type fish with white, flaky meat. Place fish in pot, cover with water and cook until fish falls from bones, about 1 hour. Pick and remove all bones. Save fish stock (There should be about 4 cups fish and 2 to 3 cups stock). In medium size pot, put fish stock and enough water to make 4 cups. Add potatoes, onions, celery and seasonings. Cook at low temperature for 45 minutes or until tender. Add butter and fish; bring to a boil. Slowly stir in milk, but do not allow to boil again. Heat until almost boiling and serve. Makes about a gallon of chowder or 12 servings. Delicious.

CRAB CHOWDER

½ cup chopped onion
½ cup chopped celery
2 tablespoons butter
1 (10½ ounce) can frozen
   potato soup
1 (8 ounce) can cream corn
2 teaspoons chopped pi-
   miento

1 bay leaf
7 to 8 ounces crabmeat,
   fresh best
½ teaspoon salt
¼ teaspoon thyme
¼ cup dry sherry
¼ teaspoon parsley flakes

Saute onions and celery in butter. Add thawed potato soup, corn, pimiento, bay leaf, crab, salt and thyme; cook gently for about 15 minutes. Just before serving stir in wine and garnish with parsley flakes.

Serves 6

CLAM CHOWDER

½ cup butter
6 tablespoons flour
46 ounces chopped clams
   with juice (about 2 cups
   juice)
2 onions finely chopped

1 bunch of celery,
   finely chopped
8 potatoes, diced
1½ cup light cream
salt

In a small pan make roux. Melt butter, add flour and cook for 5 minutes, stirring constantly. Strain clams, reserving juice. In a large pot heat juice over medium heat. When juice is hot add the roux to thicken. Boil onions, potatoes, and celery in a separate pot until tender. Add the cooked vegetables to the thickened clam broth. Add the chopped clams, the cream and seasonings. Cook 5 more minutes.

AVOCADO SALAD

2 (3 ounce) boxes lemon
  flavored gelatin
2 cups boiling water
1½ cups mashed avocados
½ cup mayonnaise
½ cup sour cream

1 tablespoon finely
  chopped onion
½ teaspoon salt
¼ teaspoon pepper
Tabasco to taste

Dissolve gelatin in boiling water; allow to cool. Combine remaining ingredients, add to gelatin and mix well. Pour into mold and refrigerate.

BEET SALAD

2 cups canned shoestring
  beets and beet juice
2 (3 ounce) packages lemon
  flavored gelatin
¾ cup boiling water

½ cup vinegar
1 teaspoon sugar
2 scant teaspoons of
  horseradish

Dissolve gelatin in boiling water. Add beet juice, vinegar, sugar and horseradish; mix well. Stir in beets. Pour into a casserole dish and chill until firm. Cut into squares to serve.

BLUEBERRY SALAD

1 (8 ounce) cream cheese
1 (3 ounce) package lemon
  flavored gelatin
1¼ cups hot water
2 cups frozen topping

1 (16 ounce) can or
  2 cups blueberries
2 (3 ounce) packages black
  cherry gelatin

Dissolve lemon gelatin in hot water; cool. Soften cream cheese; slowly mix in cooled lemon gelatin. Fold in topping mix. Pour into a lightly greased casserole dish; chill until firm. Drain blueberries. Use blueberry juice and enough water to make 3 cups of liquid. Heat liquid. Dissolve cherry gelatin in liquid, then chill until slightly thickened. Add berries, pour over cheese layer and chill until firm.

CRANBERRY SALAD

1 pound fresh whole
  cranberries
1 orange, peeled, seeded
  and cut-up
2 cups peeled, diced
  apples

2 cups chopped celery
2 cups sugar
3 cups boiling water
2 (3 ounce) packages of
  raspberry flavored gelatin

Cover fruit and celery with sugar. Refrigerate and let stand 4 hours or over night. Dissolve raspberry gelatin in boiling water; cool. Fold in fruit. Pour into a large mold and chill until ready to serve.

QUICK CRANBERRY SALAD

1 (3 ounce) package strawberry flavored gelatin
1 cup boiling water
1 (11 ounce) can crushed
  pineapple

1 (15 ounce) can whole
  berry cranberry sauce
½ cup finely, chopped celery
½ cup chopped nuts
1 tablespoon lemon juice

Dissolve gelatin in boiling water. Drain pineapple well. Combine and mix all ingredients; pour into an 8x8 inch pan. Refrigerate until congealed. Cut into squares and serve.

CUCUMBER MOUSSE

2 cucumbers
1 envelope gelatin (.25
  ounce)
½ cup cold water
1 (3 ounce) package lime
  gelatin
1¼ cups boiling water

½ cup lemon juice
2 teaspoons onion juice
¾ teaspoon salt
½ cup chopped celery
1 (9 ounce) tub frozen
  topping

Cut cucumbers in half and remove seeds. Coarsely grate, including peel. Soften plain gelatin in cold water. Dissolve lime flavored gelatin in boiling water. Add softened gelatin, lemon juice, onion juice, and salt. Chill until just the consistency of egg whites. Do not allow to become firm. Fold in cucumbers, celery, and frozen topping. Pour into a 4 cup mold that has been sprayed or lightly oiled. Chill until firm.

Serves 10 to 12

PEAR LIME SALAD

2 (3 ounce) packages lime
   flavored gelatin
¾ cup boiling water
1 tablespoon lemon juice
1 (8 ounce) carton
   cottage cheese

½ cup chopped nuts
½ cup chopped celery
½ cup mayonnaise
1 (29 ounce) can pear halves
1¾ cups boiling water

Dissolve 1 package of lime gelatin in ¾ cup boiling water.
Cool slightly and add lemon juice. Chill until partially set.
Fold in cottage cheese, nuts, celery and mayonnaise. Pour
into a 1½ quart flat casserole or oblong cake pan; chill until
set. Mix the other box of lime gelatin with 1¾ cups boiling
water; cool. Arrange pear halves on congealed first layer.
Carefully pour dissolved lime gelatin over pears. If pears float
use toothpicks to keep in place until gelatin sets. Cut with a
pear half in each serving.

CONGEALED PINK DELIGHT

1 (3 ounce) package cherry
   flavored gelatin
2 cups water
15 marshmallows
3 ounces cream cheese

1 (8 ounce) can crushed
   pineapple, drained
1 (4½ ounce) tub frozen
   topping

Dissolve gelatin in boiling water. Add marshmallows and stir
until melted. Add hot mixture to softened cream cheese; mix
well. Refrigerate until beginning to thicken but not completely
congealed. Whip with mixer. Make sure pineapple is well
drained by squeezing. Add pineapple and fold in frozen topping. Pour into 8 inch square dish. Refrigerate until firm.

CONGEALED SPINACH SALAD

2 (10-ounce) packages
   frozen,chopped spinach
1¾ teaspoons salt
3 eggs, hard boiled, chopped
¾ cups mayonnaise
1 envelope gelatin (.25
   ounce)

¼ cup cold water
1 cup consommé
4 teaspoons Worcestershire
2 teaspoons lemon juice

Cook spinach and salt without adding water. Drain well. Add eggs and mayonnaise. Soak gelatin in water. Heat consommé. Stir in softened gelatin and allow to dissolve. Add Worcestershire and lemon juice. Combine with spinach. Pour into mold and refrigerate at least 4 hours before serving.

Serves 8

QUICK ASPIC SALAD

1 (16 ounce) can stewed
   tomatoes
1 (3 ounce) package strawberry flavored gelatin

2 to 3 tablespoons
   tarragon vinegar

Chop tomatoes so there are no large pieces. Heat tomatoes and liquid. Stir in dry strawberry gelatin. Continue to stir until gelatin has completely dissovled. Add vinegar. Pour into casserole or individual molds; refrigerate. So easy and it is really tasty.

FROZEN FRUIT SALAD
A great prepare ahead recipe

1 envelope unflavored gelatin (.25 ounce)
¼ cup maraschino cherry juice
1 cup diced apricots
1 cup diced pineapple
1 cup halved seeded grapes
1 cup chopped maraschino cherries
3 tablespoons lemon juice
½ cup sugar
1 cup heavy cream
⅓ cup mayonnaise

Drain fruit. Soften gelatin in cherry juice. Heat, using double boiler, until gelatin is dissolved. Add fruits, lemon juice and sugar. Chill until syrupy. Whip cream until light and fluffy, stir in mayonnaise. Fold into fruit mixture with a wooden spoon, using an over-under motion. Spoon salad into molds, cover, and place in freezer. Unmold salad on lettuce leaves 2 hours before serving. Refrigerate until served. Waxed freezer cartons with lids make great salad molds, easily stored in freezer. This may be made weeks before needed.

Yield 8 servings.

FROZEN CRANBERRY SALAD

2 (15 ounce) cans whole
  cranberry sauce
2 (8 ounce) cream cheese
12 ounces frozen topping

1 cup chopped nuts
1 (11 ounce) can crushed
  pineapple
cherries and mint garnish

Combine all ingredients and mix well. Freeze in 24 paper-lined muffin tins. When ready to serve, remove paper, invert salad and top with a dollop of frozen topping. Garnish with half a cherry and sprig of mint.

LAYERED SALAD

1 large head lettuce,
  shredded
1 cup chopped celery
1 large green pepper,
  chopped
2 tablespoons chopped onion
1 (10 ounce) package frozen
  green peas, cooked,
  drained, cooled

2 cups mayonnaise mixed
  with 2 tablespoons sugar
1 cup Parmesan cheese
12 slices bacon, fried crisp
  and crumbled

Use flat bottom salad bowl or 2½ quart casserole dish. Layer ingredients in order given starting with lettuce and ending with bacon. Make the night before, cover and refrigerate until serving.

SALADS

HOT POTATO SALAD

¼ pound bacon
½ cup chopped onion
½ cup chopped green pepper
¼ cup vinegar
1 teaspoon salt

⅛ teaspoon pepper
1 teaspoon sugar
1 egg, beaten
4 cups cubed, cooked
  potatoes

Fry bacon until crisp. Remove and lightly cook onion and green pepper in bacon drippings. Add vinegar, salt, pepper, and sugar; stir until heated and well blended. Add a little of hot mixture to beaten egg. Pour back into skillet and blend. Add warm potatoes and crumbled bacon; toss lightly.

CORN SALAD

1 (16 ounce) can, whole
  kernel corn, drained
1 cup sliced carrots
1 cup chopped celery
1 bell pepper, chopped

2 hard boiled eggs, chopped
1 (8 ounce) package cream
  cheese with pimiento
mayonnaise

Combine all ingredients. Add enough mayonnaise to hold ingredients together.

RICE SALAD

1 onion, finely chopped
½ cup chopped parsley
½ cup cooked green peas
½ cup finely chopped red or green pepper
2 tablespoons herb flavored wine vinegar

2 teaspoons sugar
1 teaspoon dry mustard
1 teaspoon salt
pepper
2 cloves garlic, crushed
6 tablespoons olive oil
2 cups cooked rice

Mix onion, parsley, peas and bell pepper together; set aside. Combine vinegar, sugar, mustard, salt, pepper, and garlic in a jar or container with lid. Shake until mixed well. Add oil and shake until evenly mixed. Pour over vegetables and chill for at least 1 hour. When ready to serve add cold rice; toss well.

ICE BOX SLAW

1 head cabbage, shredded
1 green pepper, chopped
4 onions, diced
1 (2½ ounce) jar pimiento, chopped
2 teaspoons salt

2 cups cider vinegar
1½ cups sugar
1 teaspoon celery seed
1 teaspoon mustard seed
½ teaspoon turmeric

Mix cabbage, green pepper, onions, and pimiento in a large bowl. Combine vinegar, salt, sugar, celery seed, mustard seed and turmeric in a sauce pan; bring to a full boil. Pour over vegetables, cover and keep in the refrigerator over night before serving. Will keep almost indefinitely in the refrigerator.

FOUR BEAN SALAD

1 (16 ounce) can cut
  green beans
1 (16 ounce) can wax beans
1 (16 ounce) can red kidney
  beans
1 (16 ounce) can garbanzo
  beans
1 large onion, thinly sliced

1 green pepper, chopped
2 stalks celery, sliced
1 red bell pepper, chopped
¾ cup vinegar
¾ cup sugar
1 teaspoon salt
¼ teaspoon pepper

Drain all of the beans. Place beans, onion, green and red peppers, and celery in a large bowl. In a small sauce pan combine vinegar, sugar, salt and pepper; heat. Pour hot liquid over beans mixture. Chill over night, or at least 6 hours before serving. Will keep over a week in refrigerator.

CHICKEN MAYONNAISE DELIGHT
Excellent for luncheons

2 cups diced white
  meat chicken
1 (8 ounce) can English peas
3 hard boiled eggs, chopped
1 cup diced celery
2 tablespoons pickle relish
2 tablespoons diced olives

1 cup slivered blanched
  almonds
2 cups chicken broth
2 envelopes gelatin (.25
  ounce)
1 cup mayonnaise

Soften gelatin in chicken broth. Heat until gelatin dissolves. Cool thoroughly. Add chicken, peas, eggs,celery, relish, olives and almonds. Fold in mayonnaise last. Mold in loaf pan or oblong casserole. Slice and serve.

Serves 12

SWEETS

FRESH APPLE CAKE
Great warm, cold, plain or frosted

CAKE:
1½ cups vegetable oil
2 cups sugar
3 eggs
3 cups cake flour
½ teaspoon salt
1 teaspoon soda
2 teaspoons vanilla
1 cup chopped pecans
3 cups finely chopped apples

FROSTING:
1 stick margarine
½ cup powdered sugar
1½ cups brown sugar
1 cup granulated sugar
½ cup evaporated milk
10 to 12 marshmallows

CAKE: Combine oil, sugar, and eggs; mix well. Combine and sift together flour, salt and baking soda. Add to mixture. Add vanilla, then fold in nuts and apples. Grease and flour pan. Can be baked in a bundt or tube pan at 350 degrees for 1 hour to 1¼ hours, a 13x9x2 inch pan at 350 degrees for about 45 minutes or 3, 8 inch cake pans 35 minutes or 2 loaf pans for about 45 minutes.

FROSTING: Mix all frosting ingredients, except marshmallow, in a medium size pan; boil for about 4 minutes. Add marshmallows, stirring until melted. Beat until thick enough to spread.

BANANA NUT LAYER CAKE

CAKE:
1 stick plus 1 tablespoon
  margarine
1½ cups sugar
3 eggs
4 ripe bananas, mashed
1 tablespoon baking soda
⅓ cup plus 1 tablespoon
  buttermilk
2 teaspoons vanilla
2 cups flour
2 teaspoons baking powder
½ teaspoon salt
¾ cup nuts

FROSTING:
1 stick margarine
8 ounces cream cheese
1 box 10X powdered sugar
1 teaspoon vanilla
1 cup chopped nuts

CAKE: Cream margarine and sugar until smooth and creamy. Add eggs, one at a time, beating after each addition. In separate bowl blend mashed bananas and baking soda; add buttermilk and vanilla. Add this banana mixture to creamed mixture. Sift together flour, salt and baking powder. Sift flour into batter until smooth and well blended. Add nuts. Pour into 2 greased 9-inch cake pans and bake at 350 degrees for 20 to 25 minutes.

FROSTING: Cream margarine and cream cheese until light and fluffy. Beat in sugar and add vanilla. Frost tops and sides of layers. Sprinkle nuts on top of cake.

CARAMEL LAYER CAKE

CAKE:
¾ cup butter, softened
2 cups sugar
4 eggs
3 cups sifted cake flour
2 teaspoons baking powder
1 cup milk
1 teaspoon vanilla

CARAMEL FROSTING:
3 cups sugar
2 cups whipping cream
¼ cup butter
¼ cup light corn syrup
1 tablespoon vanilla

CAKE: Cream butter and sugar, beating until light and fluffy. Add eggs one at a time. Combine flour and baking powder. Add dry ingredients to creamed mixture alternately with milk, beginning and ending with flour mixture. Add vanilla and mix well. Pour into 2 greased and floured 9-inch cake pans. Bake at 350 degrees for 25 to 30 minutes. Cool in pans 10 minutes; remove from pans and cool completely.

FROSTING: Combine all ingredients except vanilla in a buttered heavy saucepan; cook over medium heat until a candy thermometer reaches 240 degrees (soft ball) stir often. Let cool slightly; add vanilla, and beat until spreading consistency. Spread between layers and on top and sides of cake.

COCA COLA CAKE

CAKE:
2 cups flour
2 cups sugar
1 teaspoon baking soda
1 cup margarine
1 cup Coca-Cola
3 tablespoons cocoa
1½ cups miniature
  marshamallows
½ cup buttermilk
2 eggs, beaten
1 teaspoon vanilla

ICING:
½ cup margarine
6 tablespoons Coca-Cola
1 box 10X powdered sugar
2 tablespoons cocoa
1 cup toasted chopped
  pecans
½ teaspoon vanilla

CAKE: Sift flour, sugar and soda together in a large bowl. Heat margarine, Coca-Cola and cocoa until boiling, stirring constantly. Remove from heat add marshmallows, stir until melted. Slowly pour hot mixture into flour. Stir in buttermilk, eggs and vanilla. Pour into a greased and floured sheet pan 9x13x2. Bake at 350 degrees for 40 to 45 minutes.

ICING: Sift sugar and cocoa together in a bowl. Heat margarine and Coca-Cola to a boil and pour over sugar mixture; mix well. Add nuts and vanilla. Spread on top of sheet cake.

GINGERBREAD

½ cup butter or margarine
½ cup sugar
2 eggs
2 cups sifted flour
1½ teaspoon baking soda
½ teaspoon salt

1 teaspoon ground cinnamon
1 teaspoon ground cloves
1 teaspoon ground ginger
1 cup boiling water
1 cup molasses

Cream butter and sugar together. Beat in eggs one at a time. Combine flour, soda, salt, cinnamon, cloves and ginger; stir until well mixed. Combine molasses and water. Add dry ingredients alternately with liquid, beginning and ending with flour mixture; beat well after each addition. Pour batter into a lightly greased 8x11 inch pan. Bake at 350 degree oven 35 to 40 minutes. Serve hot with Lemon Sauce.

Lemon Sauce

⅓ cup granulated sugar
1 tablespoon cornstarch
1 cup water
3 tablespoons butter

½ teaspoon grated lemon
  rind
1½ tablespoons lemon juice

Combine the sugar and cornstarch in a sauce pan. Stir in water, cook over low heat, stirring constantly, until sauce is clear and begins to thicken. Add butter, lemon juice and rind. Serve warm.

EASY CHOCOLATE SHEET CAKE

CAKE:
2 cups flour
2 cups sugar
½ teaspoon salt
1 cup margarine
1 cup water
4 tablespoons cocoa
½ cup milk
2 eggs
1 teaspoon vanilla
1 teaspoon baking soda

FROSTING:
½ cup margarine
3 tablespoons cocoa
⅓ cup milk
1 pound box powdered
    sugar
1 teaspoon vanilla
½ cup chopped pecans
    (optional)

CAKE: Combine flour, sugar and salt, in a large mixing bowl and set aside. Put margarine, water and cocoa in a sauce pan. Bring to a boil; let thicken slightly. Pour over flour mixture; mix well. Add milk, eggs, one a time, vanilla and soda last. Pour batter into greased and lightly floured 11x16x1-inch pan. Batter will be thin and easy to pour. Bake at 400 degrees for 15 to 20 minutes. Frost cake immediately on removing from oven.

FROSTING: While cake is baking place margarine, cocoa and milk in same sauce pan used for cake; boil until slightly thickened, stirring constantly. Remove from heat. Add powdered sugar, vanilla and nuts if desired; mix well. Spread on hot cake as soon as removed from oven.

CAKES

ELEGANT CHEESECAKE

CRUST:
¾ cup coarsely ground nuts
¾ cup graham cracker
  crumbs
3 tablespoons melted butter
  or margarine

TOPPING:
2 cups sour cream
¼ cup sugar
1 teaspoon vanilla

FILLING:
4 (8 ounce) packages cream
  cheese
1¼ cups sugar
4 eggs
1 tablespoon lemon juice
2 teaspoons vanilla

GLAZE:
1 pint strawberries
1 (12 ounce) jar strawberry
  or raspberry jelly
1 tablespoon cornstarch
¼ cup water
¼ cup cointreau (optional)

CAKE: Combine nuts, crumbs and butter; press firmly in bottom of 9 or 10-inch spring form pan. Beat cream cheese in mixer until light and fluffy. Beat in sugar until smooth. Add eggs, one at a time. Add lemon juice and vanilla and beat well. Spoon filling over crust. Set pan on cookie sheet and bake at 350 degrees, 10-inch pan 40 to 50 minutes, 9-inch 50 to 55 minutes. Remove from oven, let stand 15 minutes. Combine sour cream, sugar and vanilla; blend well. Spoon over top, spread to within ½ inch of edge. Return to 350 degree oven for 5 minutes. Let cake cool completely then refrigerate at least 24 hours (better if 2 days).

GLAZE: A couple hours before serving wash and hull berries; dry. Combine jelly with cornstarch in sauce pan and mix well. Add remaining jelly, water and Cointreau. Cook over medium heat, stir until thickens and clears, (about 5 minutes). Cool. Using knife loosen cake from pan; remove spring form. Arrange berries on top of cake spoon glaze over berries and drip down sides. Return to refrigerator.

MISSISSIPPI MUD CAKE

CAKE:
2 cups sugar
2 sticks butter or margarine
4 eggs
1½ cups flour
⅓ cup cocoa
⅛ teaspoon salt
1½ cups chopped pecans
1 teaspoon vanilla
Miniature marshmallows
   to cover cake

FROSTING:
1 stick margarine (melted)
⅓ cup evaporated milk
⅓ cup cocoa
1 pound box powdered sugar
1 teaspoon vanilla
1 cup chopped nuts

CAKE: Cream sugar and butter. Add eggs one at a time and beat well. Sift flour, cocoa and salt together and add to creamed mixture mixing well. Add vanilla and nuts. Pour into a greased and floured 13x9-inch pan and bake at 300 or 350 degrees for 35 minutes. Remove from oven and spread marshmallows on top. Return to oven until marshmallows have melted about 10 minutes. Cool and frost.

FROSTING: Combine margarine, milk and cocoa in saucepan. Cook on low heat until melted. Add sugar and mix until smooth. Add vanilla and nuts. Spread on cake.

CHOCOLATE BROWNIE CHEESECAKE

4 ounces semi-sweet
chocolate
5 tablespoons butter or
margarine, divided
3 eggs
1 cup sugar, divided
½ teaspoon baking powder
¼ teaspoon salt

½ cup flour
½ cup chopped nuts
¼ teaspoon almond extract
1 teaspoon vanilla
3 ounces cream cheese
1 tablespoon flour
½ teaspoon vanilla

Melt chocolate and 3 tablespoons of the butter in a double
boiler. Set aside to cool. Beat 2 of the eggs together; add
¾ cup of the sugar gradually until well mixed. After the
chocolate mixture has cooled add it to the eggs; stir well.
Mix baking powder, salt, ½ cup flour and nuts together; add
to chocolate mixture. Stir in almond and 1 teaspoon vanilla;
set aside. Blend cream cheese and remaining 2 tablespoons
of butter. Add remaining ¼ cup sugar, 1 egg, 1 tablespoon
flour and ½ teaspoon vanilla; mix well. Grease and line
an 8 inch spring form pan with waxed paper. Pour ⅔ of
chocolate mixture in pan. Spread the cream cheese mixture
over the chocolate. Spoon remaining chocolate mixture over
cheese. Run a knife through layers to marblelize two
mixtures. Bake in a 350 degree oven for 35 minutes or until
pick inserted in center comes out clean. Cool and place in
refrigerator over night.

ROTTEN CAKE
Coconut Delight

1 (18½ ounce) yellow cake
  mix 2 layer size

FROSTING:
1 pint sour cream, divided
1 cup sugar

1 teaspoon vanilla
1 (9 ounce) carton frozen
  non-dairy topping
2 (6 ounce) packages frozen
  coconut

Bake cake as directed on box. Cool and slice layers in half to make 4 thin layers. Combine 1 cup sour cream, sugar, vanilla and 1 package of coconut. Spread between layers. Combine 1 cup sour cream and thawed topping mix. Spread on top and sides of cake. Sprinkle with remaining coconut. Place in airtight container and refrigerate for 3 days (leave to "Rot".) Outstanding!!

ITALIAN CREAM CAKE

2 cups sugar
½ cup butter
½ cup shortening
5 eggs, separated
2 cups flour
½ teaspoon salt
1 teaspoon soda
1 cup buttermilk
1 teaspoon vanilla
2 cups coconut
1 cup chopped pecans

CREAM CHEESE ICING
1 (8 ounce) package cream
  cheese
¼ cup butter, softened
½ teaspoon vanilla
1 pound box confectioners
  sugar

Cream sugar, butter and shortening. Add egg yolks one at a time beating well after each addition. Sift flour, salt, and soda together. Add dry ingredients alternately with buttermilk. Add vanilla, coconut and nuts. Beat egg whites until stiff; fold into batter. Pour batter into 3 greased and floured 8 inch cake pans. Bake at 350 degrees for 20 to 30 minutes. Cool a few minutes in pan, then invert on rack and remove from pan to cool. Frost layers and sides with cream cheese icing.

CREAM CHEESE ICING: Cream butter and cheese; add vanilla. Mix in powdered sugar. Beat until smooth.

HUMMINGBIRD CAKE

CAKE:
3 cups flour
2 cups sugar
1 teaspoon soda
1 teaspoon salt
1 teaspoon cinnamon
3 eggs, beaten
1 cup vegetable oil
1½ teaspoons vanilla
1 cup chopped nuts
1 (8 ounce) can crushed
   pineapple, with juice
2 cups chopped bananas

FROSTING:
1 (8 ounce) package
   cream cheese
1 stick margarine or butter
1 (16 ounce) box powdered
   sugar
1 teaspoon vanilla
½ cup chopped nuts

CAKE: Mix flour, sugar, soda, salt and cinnamon and set aside. Beat eggs and add vegetable oil. Stir egg mixture into dry ingredients. Stir until well mixed. Add vanilla, nuts, pineapple, with juice and bananas. Pour into 3 greased and floured 9-inch pans. Bake at 350 degrees for 25 to 30 minutes. Cool.

FROSTING: Set cream cheese and butter out to soften; combine and beat until smooth. Add powdered sugar and vanilla. Beat until light and fluffy. Frost cake and sprinkle chopped nuts on top.

LANE CAKE

CAKE:
1 cup butter or margarine
2 cups sugar
1 teaspoon vanilla
3¼ cups flour
3½ teaspoons baking
  powder
1 cup milk
8 egg whites

WHITE FLUFFY FROSTING:
1 cup sugar
⅓ cup water
Dash of cream of tartar
Dash of salt
2 egg whites
1 teaspoon vanilla

FILLING:
8 egg yolks
1 cup sugar
½ cup butter or margarine
1 cup chopped nuts
1 cup raisins
½ cup marachino cherries,
  cut
1 cup coconut
¼ to ⅓ cup wine, bourbon, or
  liqueur

CAKE: Cream butter and sugar until light and smooth, add vanilla. Sift flour and baking powder together. Add to creamed mixture alternately with milk, beating well after each addition. Fold in egg whites. Pour into 3 greased and floured 9-inch pans and bake at 350 degrees for 20 to 25 minutes or until done. Cool in pans 10 minutes; remove from pans and cool completely.

FILLING: Combine yolks, sugar and butter in saucepan over low heat. Stir over low heat until mixture thickens. Remove from heat and add remaining ingredients. Cool to room temperature. Spread on tops of layers only.

FROSTING: In sauce pan combine sugar, water, cream of tartar and salt. Bring to boil. Beat egg whites and slowly add syrup. Add vanilla. Beat about 7 minutes until peaks form. Spread around side of cake.

PISTACHIO CAKE

CAKE:
1 box white cake mix
  (2 layer size)
¾ cup vegetable oil
¾ cup water
4 eggs
1 (3 ounce) box Pistachio
  instant pudding
½ cup chopped nuts

GLAZE:
½ cup hot water
1 tablespoon butter, melted
2 cups powdered sugar
½ teaspoon vanilla

CAKE: Combine cake mix, oil, water, eggs and pudding mix. Beat about 4 minutes at medium speed. Pour into greased and floured 9x13x2-inch pan. Sprinkle top with nuts. Bake at 350 degrees for 35 to 40 minutes.

GLAZE: Place water, butter, powdered sugar and vanilla in small bowl and beat with a fork. While cake is still hot punch holes with a fork over the entire top. Spoon icing over cake allowing it to run down into holes. Pry holes open if necessary to insure that the icing runs into cake. Is a pretty green, stays moist and is a real favorite.

PINEAPPLE UPSIDE-DOWN CAKE

½ cup butter or margarine
1 cup brown sugar (packed)
1 (15 ounce) can pineapple
  slices
½ cup chopped pecans
3 eggs, separated

1 cup sugar
1 teaspoon vanilla
1 cup flour
1 teaspoon baking powder
½ teaspoon salt
6 to 8 Maraschino cherries

Melt butter in a 9-inch iron skillet. Add brown sugar and stir until sugar melts. Drain pineapple, reserving ⅓ cup of juice. Arrange pineapple slices in a single layer on top of brown sugar mixture (7 or 8 slices). Sprinkle pecans over pineapple. Beat egg yolks until thick and lemon colored. Gradually beat in sugar; blend well. Beat in vanilla and ⅓ cup of pineapple juice. Combine flour, baking powder and salt; add to batter. Beat egg whites until stiff peaks form; fold into batter. Spoon batter into skillet, over pineapple and nuts. Bake at 350 degrees for 40 to 45 minutes or until center springs back when lightly touched. Allow 20 minutes; invert onto serving plate. Place cherries in center of pineapple slices.

POUND CAKES

Grandmothers traditional pound cakes got their name from the ingredients - there was a pound of butter, a pound of eggs, a pound of sugar and a pound of flour plus a little salt and a teaspoon of vanilla. They were delicious! Here are some delightful variations.

OLD-FASHIONED POUND CAKE

1½ cups butter or margarine
3 cups sugar
5 eggs
1 teaspoon vanilla
3 cups flour
½ teaspoon baking powder
1 cup milk

Cream butter and sugar. Add eggs, one at a time, beating well after each; add vanilla. Combine flour and baking powder. Alternately add flour and milk, beginning and ending with flour. Pour into a greased and floured tube pan. Bake at 350 degrees for 1 hour and 15 minutes or until pick inserted in center comes out clean.

SOUR CREAM POUND CAKE

1 cup butter or margarine
3 cups sugar
6 eggs
3 cups flour
¼ teaspoon soda
1 cup sour cream
1 teaspoon vanilla

Cream butter and sugar together until light and fluffy. Add eggs, one at a time, beating well after each. Sift flour and baking soda together. Add flour alternately with sour cream, beginning and ending with flour; add vanilla. Pour into a greased and floured tube or bundt pan. Bake at 325 degrees for 1 hour and 30 minutes until pick inserted in center comes out clean.

BROWN SUGAR POUND CAKE

1 cup butter
½ cup margarine
1 pound light brown sugar
1 cup white sugar
5 eggs
3 cups sifted flour
¼ teaspoon salt
1 teaspoon baking powder
1 cup milk

1 teaspoon vanilla
1 cup chopped nuts
FROSTING:
2 tablespoons butter
1 cup sifted powdered
    sugar
6 tablespoons cream
½ teaspoon vanilla
½ cup chopped nuts

Cream butter and margarine. Gradually add sugars and beat until light and fluffy. Add eggs one at a time; beat well after each. Whisk sifted flour, salt and baking powder together. Add to creamed mixture alternately with milk, beginning and ending with flour. Add vanilla; mix well. Stir in pecans. Pour batter into a greased and floured tube pan. Bake at 350 degrees for 1 hour and 15 minutes, or when pick inserted in cake comes out clean. Cool 10 to 15 minutes in pan. Remove and add frosting while still warm.

FROSTING: Cream butter, beat in powdered sugar and gradually add cream and vanilla. Stir in nuts and pour over cake.

WALDORF CAKE

CAKE:
½ cup butter or margarine
1½ cups sugar
2 eggs
1 teaspoon vanilla
2 tablespoons cocoa
2 (1 ounce) bottles red food
  coloring
2¼ cups sifted flour
½ teaspoon salt
1 cup buttermilk
1 teaspoon soda
1 tablespoon vinegar

WALDORF ICING:
½ cup flour
1½ cups milk
1½ cups butter
1½ cups powdered sugar
1½ teaspoons vanilla

CAKE: Cream butter and sugar. Add eggs one at a time; add vanilla. Make a paste of cocoa and food coloring; beat into mixture. Combine flour and salt; add to mixture alternately with buttermilk. Blend soda and vinegar and add to batter. Pour into greased and floured 9-inch pans. (Make 4 very thin layers or 2 layers and split to make 4 after cake has cooled.)

ICING: Cook flour and milk over low heat until pasty; cool. Cream sugar and butter, add vanilla and paste. Whip in mixer until like whipped cream. Spread between layers, top and sides.

FUDGE

2 cups sugar	1 tablespoon butter
1 cup milk	pinch salt
2 ounces chocolate	⅓ teaspoon vanilla

Heat milk separately, add melted chocolate. Pour over sugar, stir well. Cook in heavy pan. Stir until boils, boil gently then only fold occasionally. Cook to 230. Remove from heat, add butter, salt, and vanilla. Cool and beat vigorously. Add chopped nuts and pour on greased pan or plate.

CHOCOLATE TOFFEE BARS

Graham Crackers	12 ounces milk chocolate
1 cup margarine	chips or candy bars
1 cup brown sugar	1 cup finely chopped
	pecans

Break crackers apart and arrange on a 10x15 inch foil lined jelly roll pan. Cover entire pan. Melt margarine and sugar and bring to a boil. Boil 3 minutes. Remove from heat and pour boiling mixture over crackers. Bake for 5 minutes at 400 degrees. Remove from oven and sprinkle chocolate chips over top at once. As chocolate melts, spread evenly over top. Sprinkle top with nuts while chocolate soft. Cool and cut.

Yield: Approximately 6 dozen.

DIVINITY

2½ cups sugar
½ cup water
½ cup light corn syrup
⅛ teaspoon salt

2 egg whites
1 teaspoon vanilla
1 cup finely chopped nuts

Combine sugar, water and syrup in a large heavy saucepan. Bring to a boil, stirring only until sugar is dissolved. Continue boiling, without stirring until syrup reaches 240 degrees. A few minutes before syrup is ready combine egg whites and salt. Beat until stiff. Slowly pour in a thin stream ½ of syrup into whites, while beating. Return remaining syrup to heat and boil until it reaches 260 degrees. Add this half slowly to mixture while beating. Continue to beat until it loses gloss. Add vanilla and fold in nuts. Drop by tablespoon onto waxed paper. Swirl to form peak. Decorate with halved candied cherries.

OLD-FASHIONED PEANUT BRITTLE

3 cups sugar
½ cup water
1 cup white corn syrup
3 cups raw peanuts

2 tablespoons soda
4 tablespoons margarine
1 teaspoon vanilla

Grease cookie sheets or 2 large pieces of aluminum foil. Combine and heat sugar, water and syrup in a large heavy sauce pan. Stir until sugar dissolves. Boil on medium to medium high until syrup spins a thread, 230 to 235 degrees on a candy thermometer; add peanuts. Continue to boil, stirring constantly, until syrup reaches the hard crack stage 300 to 305 degrees on your thermometer. Syrup will be a golden brown and peanuts will pop. Remove from heat. Add soda, margarine and vanilla; stir until margarine melts. Pour quickly onto foil or pans. As mixture begins to cool pull to stretch until thin. When cool break into pieces.

Yield: 2½ to 3 lbs.

POPCORN BALLS

4 quarts popped corn
1 cup sugar
1 cup light corn syrup
¼ cup water

¼ teaspoon salt
3 tablespoons margarine
1 teaspoon vanilla

Combine sugar, syrup, water, salt and margarine in small sauce pan. Cook over medium heat, stirring until sugar dissolves and mixture boils. Continue cooking, without stirring, until it reaches 250 degrees on candy thermometer (hard-ball stage). Remove from heat and add vanilla. Pour slowly over popped corn in large bowl and mix to coat all kernels. Work quickly and shape into 4-inch balls. (As you are working with part of corn you can keep remaining in oven at 200 degrees to stay warm and pliable). Place square of waxed paper under each ball.

Yield: 7 or 8 balls

LOUISIANA PRALINES

1½ cups granulated sugar
1½ cups light brown sugar,
   firmly packed
¼ cup corn syrup
⅛ teaspoon salt

1 cup evaporated milk
4 tablespoons margarine
1 teaspoon vanilla
1½ cups broken pecans

Combine the sugars, corn syrup, salt, milk and margarine in a large, heavy saucepan. Cook over medium heat stirring constantly until sugar is dissolved. Stir frequently until mixture reaches 236 degrees on candy thermometer or until it forms a soft ball when dropped in cold water. Remove from heat and cool for 2 or 3 minutes. Add vanilla and nuts; beat with wooden spoon until mixture begins to thicken. Quickly drop by spoonfuls onto greased foil. Allow to cool.

PRALINES

3 cups brown sugar, packed
1 cup heavy cream
¼ teaspoon salt

¼ cup butter
2 teaspoons vanilla
2½ cups pecan pieces

Combine sugar, cream and salt in a heavy large sauce pan. Heat and stir until sugar dissolves. Bring to a boil; boil until thermometer reaches 238 degrees. Remove from heat, add butter and cool to 200 degrees without stirring. Add vanilla and pecans. Beat until begins to thicken. Drop mixture by teaspoonfuls onto buttered waxed paper.

COOKIES

CHOCOLATE CHIP-OATMEAL COOKIES

1½ cups flour
1 teaspoon soda
1 teaspoon salt
1 cup margarine
¾ cup brown sugar
¾ cup white sugar
2 eggs

1 teaspoon hot water
1 teaspoon vanilla
1 (12 ounce) bag chocolate
   morsels
1 cup chopped nuts
2 cups oatmeal

Sift flour, soda and salt and set aside. Cream margarine and sugars. Add eggs one at a time, beating well. Add hot water, vanilla and then flour mixture. Mix well. Stir in chocolate drops, nuts and oatmeal. Drop on greased cookie sheet and bake at 350 degrees 10 to 12 minutes.

Yield: 5 dozen

OLD-FASHIONED OATMEAL COOKIES

⅔ cup margarine or butter
1 cup sugar
2 eggs
1½ cups flour
½ teaspoon baking powder
½ teaspoon baking soda
⅔ cup buttermilk

1 teaspoon vanilla
½ teaspoon allspice
½ teaspoon cinnamon
1 cup raisins
1 cup chopped nuts
2 cups regular rolled oats

Cream butter and sugar. Beat eggs and add to butter mixture. Sift flour, baking powder and soda together and add to cream mixture. Add buttermilk, mix well and add vanilla, allspice and cinnamon. Fold in oatmeal, raisins and nuts. Will be a stiff batter. Drop by teaspoonfuls onto greased baking sheet. Bake at 400 degrees for 8 to 10 minutes or until cookies are light brown.

Yield: 5 dozen

SUGAR COOKIES
Cookie Cutter Delight

1 cup butter	2½ cups flour
1 cup granulated sugar	½ teaspoon baking powder
½ cup sifted confectioners sugar	¼ teaspoon salt
1 egg	Red and green colored sugar crystals, optional
1 teaspoon vanilla	

Beat together butter and sugars until light and fluffy. Blend in egg and vanilla. Combine flour, baking powder, and salt; add to butter mixture, mixing until well blended. Roll out on lightly floured surface ⅛ inch thick; cut with floured cookie cutters. Sprinkle with red and green colored sugar crystals if desired. Bake on ungreased cookie sheet in 350 degree oven. For 3-inch cookies bake 8 to 10 minutes or until edges are lightly browned.

Yield: 5 dozen

MELT-IN-YOUR MOUTH COOKIES

½ cup butter	¾ cup flour
1 cup brown sugar	1 teaspoon baking powder
1 teaspoon vanilla	½ teaspoon salt
1 egg	½ cup finely chopped nuts

Cream butter. Add sugar, vanilla and egg. Beat until light. Add dry ingredients and nuts. Drop scant teaspoon on ungreased cookie sheet. Bake in preheated 400 degree oven for 5 minutes. Cool ½ minute and remove to wire racks to cool.

Yield: 3 dozen

COOKIES

OLD FASHIONED ICE BOX COOKIES

3 cups flour
1 teaspoon baking powder
¼ teaspoon salt
1½ cups sugar

1 cup margarine
3 eggs
1 teaspoon vanilla
½ cup chopped nuts

Sift flour, baking powder, salt and sugar together. Add margarine and mix well; add eggs, vanilla and nuts. Form into rolls 8x2; wrap in waxed paper and refrigerate. Slice and place on cookie sheet. Bake 375 degrees 8 minutes.

Yield: 6 dozen

SCONES

Scones are made like biscuits only sweeter and more flaky. Scones were first brought to America by the Scottish settlers.

2 cups all-purpose flour
1 teaspoon salt
2½ teaspoons baking
  powder
2 tablespoons sugar

½ cup margarine
2 eggs, beaten
¾ cup milk or cream

Sift or stir dry ingredients together in a large bowl. Cut in margarine with pastry blender; add eggs and enough milk to form a soft dough. Turn onto a floured surface and knead lightly. Divide dough in half and roll or press each into a circle ½-inch thick. With a sharp knife cut each into 6 wedges. Place on a greased baking sheet. Brush tops with margarine and sprinkle with sugar. Bake at 400 degrees 10 to 12 minutes. If you like a sweeter taste, top with a powdered sugar glaze.

Yield: 12 scones

SNOWBALLS

½ pound butter
5 tablespoons sugar
½ teaspoon salt

2 cups flour
1 cup finely chopped pecans
Powdered sugar

Soften butter, add sugar and mix well. Add salt, flour and nuts. Roll into small balls. Bake at 325 degrees for 25 minutes. Roll in powdered sugar.

PETTICOAT TAILS

2 sticks softened butter
1 cup sifted powdered sugar
1 teaspoon vanilla (or almond)

2½ cups sifted flour
¼ teaspoon salt

Cream butter and sugar. Add vanilla. Sift flour and salt and mix in by hand. Mold into 2 smooth rolls 2 inches in diameter. Roll in waxed paper and chill several hours or overnight. Cut into thin slices. Place on ungreased cookie sheet and bake 8 to 10 minutes at 400 degrees.

Yield: 6 dozen 2-inch cookies

PEANUT BUTTER COOKIES

1 cup margarine
1 cup smooth peanut butter
1 cup sugar
1 cup brown sugar, packed

3 eggs
3 cups flour
2 teaspoons baking soda
¼ teaspoon salt

Cream margarine, peanut butter and both sugars. Add eggs, one at a time, beating well after each. Sift flour, baking soda and salt together; add to creamed mixture. Roll dough into small balls, about 1½ inches. Place on a ungreased cookie sheet and flatten. Using a fork makes a nice design. Bake in a 375 degree oven for 10 to 15 minutes.

Yields 3 1/2 dozen

PEANUT BUTTER KISSES

1 cup creamy peanut butter
1½ sticks margarine
½ cup firmly packed dark
   brown sugar
2 eggs
2½ cups flour

½ teaspoon baking powder
¼ teaspoon salt
About 48 milk chocolate
   candies (chocolate kisses or
   silver bells)

Beat peanut butter, margarine and sugar. Add eggs. Combine flour, baking powder and salt. Add to mixture. Beat at low speed until well blended. Roll dough into ball; wrap with plastic wrap and refrigerate until easy to handle (about 1 hour). Shape dough into balls; place 2 inches apart on ungreased cookie sheet. Press top and flatten with fork. Bake at 375 degrees for 15 minutes or until golden. Remove from oven and quickly press a candy into center of each cookie.

Yield: 4 dozen

FRUIT CAKE COOKIES

1 (16 ounce) package candied cherries, chopped
1 (16 ounce) package green candied pineapple, chopped
3 cups chopped nuts
2 cups raisins
3 cups flour, divided
1 teaspoon baking soda
¼ teaspoon salt
1 teaspoon cinnamon
1 teaspoon nutmeg
1 teaspoon ground cloves
1 stick margarine
1 cup brown sugar, firmly packed
4 eggs
½ cup bourbon (optional)
3 tablespoons milk

Mix ½ cup flour with cherries, pineapple, nuts and raisins. Toss to coat. Combine 2½ cups flour, soda, salt, cinnamon, nutmeg and cloves; set aside. Soften margarine and beat in sugar. Continue beating until light and fluffy. Add eggs and mix well. Add flour mixture gradually. Add milk and bourbon if desired. Stir in fruit mixture. Drop by teaspoonfuls on lightly greased cookie sheet. Bake 300 degrees for 20 minutes.

Yield: 9 dozen

FORGOTTEN COOKIES

2 egg whites
½ teaspoon cream of tartar
Pinch of salt
⅔ cup sugar
1 teaspoon vanilla
½ cup chocolate morsels
½ cup chopped nuts

Beat egg whites until foamy; add cream of tartar and salt. Beat in sugar, until sugar dissolves and whites are stiff. Fold in vanilla, chocolate drops, and nuts. Drop by teaspoon on greased cookie sheet. (Cookies will not spread). Place cookies in oven preheated to 400 degrees. Immediately turn off oven and "forget cookies" until morning or at least 4 hours.

POTATO CHIP COOKIES

1 cup margarine
½ cup sugar
1 teaspoon vanilla

1½ cups sifted flour
½ cup crushed potato chips

Cream margarine and sugar. Beat in vanilla, flour and chips. Drop by teaspoonfuls on an ungreased cookie sheet. Bake at 350 degrees for 10 to 12 minutes.

Yield: 4 dozen

RUM BALLS

2 tablespoons corn syrup
¼ cup rum
1 cup powdered sugar
1 cup finely chopped pecans

2 tablespoons cocoa
1 (12 ounce) box vanilla
  wafers, finely crushed

Combine all ingredients. Form into balls. Roll in powdered sugar. Store in refrigerator.

HAYSTACKS

12 ounces butterscotch chips
6 ounces chocolate chips

1 (5 ounce) can Chinese
  noodles
½ cup chopped peanuts

Melt chips in double boiler. Stir in Chinese noodles and nuts. Drop by spoonfuls on waxed paper.

THIMBLE COOKIES

1 cup margarine or butter
½ cup brown sugar
2 eggs, separated
½ teaspoon vanilla
2 cups flour
¼ teaspoon salt
1 cup finely chopped pecans
Chocolate Frosting or
Strawberry Preserves

FROSTING:
¼ cup milk
4 tablespoons cocoa
1 cup sugar
4 tablespoons margarine
½ teaspoon vanilla

Cream margarine and sugar. Add egg yolks that have been beaten slightly; add vanilla. Combine flour and salt; add to creamed mixture. Chill dough. Shape dough into small balls. Dip each ball into the slightly beaten egg whites, then roll in chopped nuts. Place on a greased cookie sheet and bake at 375 degrees for 15 minutes. Remove from oven, make indention in top of each cookie with a thimble or other small round object. Put about ½ teaspoon of chocolate frosting in each cookie.

CHOCOLATE FROSTING: Combine milk, cocoa and sugar in small saucepan. Bring to a boil and boil 2 minutes; stir constantly. Remove from heat, add margarine and vanilla. Beat until cools slightly.

If using strawberry preserves for filling -bake cookies for 8 minutes - remove from oven place small amount of preserves in each hole, then return to oven and bake 7 more minutes.

7 LAYER COOKIES

1 stick butter or margarine
1½ cups graham cracker
  crumbs
1 (3½ ounce) can flaked
  coconut
1 cup chopped pecans

1 (6 ounce) package of
  chocolate chips
1 (6 ounce) package of
  butterscotch chips
1 (14 ounce) can condensed
  milk

Melt margarine in 13x9x2 inch pan or baking dish. Sprinkle graham cracker crumbs evenly in bottom of pan. Follow with layer of coconut, chocolate chips, butterscotch chips and nuts. Pat down each layer. Top with condensed milk. With back of spoon pack the mixture down. Let this stand for a few minutes so the milk can be absorbed in the layers. Bake at 350 degrees for 25 minutes (or until nuts just begin to brown). Cool before cutting in bars. (Cuts better if put in refrigerator).

BROWNIES

2 cups flour
½ teaspoon salt
2 cups sugar
1 cup margarine
4 tablespoons cocoa or
   4 ounces unsweetened
   chocolate
4 eggs, beaten
1 teaspoon vanilla

FROSTING:
½ cup margarine
4 tablespoons cocoa
⅓ cup milk
1 pound box powdered sugar
1 teaspoon vanilla
½ cup chopped nut (optional)

Sift together flour, salt and sugar into large mixing bowl. Place margarine and chocolate in top of double boiler, cook until chocolate melts and is mixed well. Pour hot liquid into dry ingredients while beating at medium speed. Add eggs and vanilla. Pour into a well-greased 13x9x2-inch pan. Bake for 20 minutes at 400 degrees. Remove from oven and spread with frosting while hot.

FROSTING: While brownies are baking place margarine, cocoa and milk in same double boiler. Boil until slightly thickened, stirring constantly. Remove from heat and add powdered sugar, vanilla and nuts if desired. Mix well. Spread on brownies as soon as they are removed from oven.

Yield: 36

BUTTERSCOTCH BROWNIES

1 stick butter or margarine
2 cups brown sugar, packed
2 eggs
1 teaspoon vanilla
2 cups flour
1 teaspoon baking powder
¼ teaspoon soda
½ teaspoon salt
½ cup chopped pecans
1 (6 ounce) package
   semi-sweet butterscotch
   morsels

Cream margarine and sugar until light and fluffy. Add eggs one at a time, beating well after each. Add vanilla. Combine flour, baking powder, soda and salt; add to creamed mixture, mixing until smooth. Pour into greased 13x9-inch pan. Sprinkle pecans and butterscotch chips over top. Bake at 350 degrees for 30 to 35 minutes. Cut into bars while warm.

Yield: 36

CINNAMON STICKS

1½ sticks margarine
1 cup sugar
1 egg, separated
2 cups flour
2 tablespoons cinnamon
½ teaspoon salt
1 cup chopped nuts

Mix butter and sugar together with a spoon. Add egg yolk and stir well. Sift flour, cinnamon and salt together. Add to creamed mixture. Mix well and knead with hands. Pat out on cookie sheet or oblong cake pan. Beat egg white slightly and spread over dough. Sprinkle nuts over top and press lightly into dough. Bake at 325 degrees for 30 minutes. While still warm cut into squares or oblong strips.

Yield: 3 dozen

PECAN PIE BARS

1 (2 layer) yellow cake mix
½ stick margarine, melted
4 eggs
½ cup brown sugar

1½ cups corn syrup
1 teaspoon vanilla
1 cup chopped pecans

Measure ⅔ cup cake mix and set aside. Combine remaining cake mix, melted margarine and one egg. Mix until crumbly. Press in bottom of greased 13x9x2-inch pan. Bake until light brown, 15 to 20 minutes. While crust is baking combine the remaining cake mix with sugar, syrup, vanilla and 3 eggs. Beat until well blended. Remove crust from oven. Pour filling over top and sprinkle with chopped nuts. Return to 350 degree oven and bake for 30 to 35 minutes. Cool and cut into bars.

LUSCIOUS LEMON BARS

2 sticks margarine
½ cup powdered sugar
2½ cups flour, divided
4 eggs

2 cups sugar
½ teaspoon baking powder
6 tablespoons lemon juice

Melt margarine and mix with sugar and 2 cups flour. Press into 9x13-inch pan and bake 15 to 20 minutes at 350 degrees. While baking prepare lemon layer. Beat eggs until fluffy. Add sugar and mix well. Add ½ cup flour, baking powder and lemon juice and mix until blended. Pour over cookie layer and return to 350 degree oven for 25 minutes or until set. Cool and cut into squares.

TEA TIME TASSIES

3 ounces cream cheese
½ cup butter
1 cup flour

Filling:
1 tablespoon butter
1 egg, beaten
1 teaspoon vanilla
¾ cup brown sugar
⅔ cup finely chopped pecans

Soften and combine cream cheese and butter. Mix in flour; place in refrigerator to chill. Roll into 24 small balls; press into tiny muffin tins to form pie shells. Filling: Combine butter, egg, vanilla and sugar, mix well. Stir in nuts. Spoon into small, unbaked shells. Bake at 325 degrees for 25 minutes.

CHOCOLATE CHIP PANCAKES
Childrens delight

1½ cup flour
¼ cup cocoa powder
3 tablespoon sugar
1 tablespoon baking powder
½ teaspoon salt

1 egg, slightly beaten
1¼ cups milk
3 tablespoons butter, melted
½ cup semi-sweet chocolate chips

Combine flour, cocoa, sugar, baking powder and salt together. Stir together the egg, milk and melted butter. Stir the liquid mixture into the dry ingredients. Do not over mix; stir just until smooth. Grease the insides of several metal cookie cutters. Place cutters on a greased skillet over medium heat. Fill about ¼ full. When bubbles begin to form sprinkle tops with chocolate chips. When top sets and is covered with bubbles remove cutters and carefully turn to other side. Remove from skillet when done and sprinkle with powder sugar.

APPLE DELIGHT

¾ cup butter or margarine
1 (18 ounce) box yellow cake mix, 2 layer size
2½ cups sliced apples or a (20 ounce) can pie sliced apples, drained

½ cup granulated sugar
1 teaspoon cinnamon
¼ teaspoon nutmeg
1 cup sour cream
2 egg yolks

Cut butter into cake mix until crumbly. Press into bottom and sides of a 13x9x2 inch baking dish. Bake 10 minutes. Arrange apples on warm crust. Combine sugar, cinnamon and nutmeg; sprinkle over apples. Mix sour cream and egg yolks; spread over apples. Topping will not completely cover apples. Bake in a 350 degree oven for 25 minutes.

APPLE STRUDEL

6 large or 8 medium apples
½ teaspoon cinnamon
1 cup granulated sugar
½ cup brown sugar

½ cup margarine
1 cup flour
1 cup chopped pecans

Peel and slice apples, place in buttered baking pan (9x13"). Mix cinnamon and granulated sugar. Sprinkle over apples. Cream brown sugar and margarine. Add flour and nuts and pour over thinly sliced apples. Bake at 350 degrees for 30 to 40 minutes.

OLD FASHION BAKED CUSTARD

3 eggs
½ cup sugar
2 cups milk

½ teaspoon vanilla
pinch of salt

Beat eggs just until mixed; add sugar. Whisk or stir until well mixed. Add milk, vanilla and salt. Pour into individual custard cups. Place cups in pan of hot water and bake at 350 degrees for 30 minutes or until knife inserted in center comes out clean.

ATLANTA FLAN

½ cup sugar
1 (8 ounce) package
   cream cheese, softened
3 slices white bread
1 (14 ounce) can
   sweetened condensed milk
4 eggs

1 cup water
⅔ cup evaporated milk
3 tablespoons butter or
   margarine, melted
1 teaspoon vanilla

Sprinkle sugar in the bottom of a 9 inch round cake pan. Place pan over medium heat until sugar melts and turns a light brown. You will need to shake pan occasionally. Set aside to cool. Cut softened cheese into small pieces and place in blender. Add bread slices that have been torn into small pieces. Add remaining ingredients; the condensed milk, eggs, water, evaporated milk, butter and vanilla. Process until smooth. Pour over caramelized sugar in cake pan. Place cake pan in a large flat pan. Add hot water to larger pan to about 1 inch depth. Bake uncovered in a 350 degree oven for 55 minutes or until knife inserted in center comes out clean. Remove cake pan from hot water and allow to cool at least 30 minutes. Loosen sides with wet knife and invert flan onto serving dish.

Serves 6

OLD FASHIONED BREAD PUDDING

2 cups milk, scalded
4 tablespoons margarine
2 eggs, lightly beaten
¾ cup sugar
¼ teaspoon salt

1 teaspoon ground cinnamon
1 teaspoon vanilla
5 cups soft bread cubes
   (about 9 slices)
½ cup raisins, optional

Vanilla Sauce

⅓ cup sugar
¼ teaspoon salt
2 tablespoons cornstarch

1⅔ cups water
3 tablespoons margarine
2 teaspoons vanilla

Combine hot milk and margarine. When melted, add to beaten eggs. Add sugar, salt, cinnamon, and vanilla; mix well. Gently stir in bread and raisins if desired. Pour into a greased 2 quart casserole or baking pan. Bake at 350 degrees for 40 to 45 minutes.

Sauce: Combine sugar, salt and cornstarch in a sauce pan. Add water and cook until it begins to thicken, 3 or 4 minutes. Add margarine and vanilla. Serve both warm.

For a different taste add ½ teaspoon ground nutmeg to pudding and ¼ teaspoon nutmeg to sauce.

CHOCOLATE DELIGHT

1 cup flour
½ cup margarine
1 cup ground pecans
8 ounces cream cheese
1 (9 ounce) carton frozen
  topping, divided

1 cup powdered sugar
1 (3½ ounce) instant
  chocolate pudding mix
1 (3½ ounce) instant vanilla
  pudding mix
3 cups milk

Melt margarine, add flour and nuts; mix well. Press into bottom of 2-quart casserole. Bake at 350 degrees for 18 to 20 minutes. Allow to cool. Mix cream cheese, 1 cup frozen topping and powdered sugar. Blend and spread on cooled crust. Combine pudding mixes and milk; beat a couple minutes until thickens, then pour on cream cheese layer. Top with remaining topping. Chill 6 hours. Can be cut and served in squares or spooned.

POTS DE CREME

8 ounces sweet baking
  chocolate
1 cup whipping cream

4 egg yolks
1 teaspoon vanilla
Whipped cream for garnishing

Have water in double boiler boiling. Reduce heat to low; add chocolate. When chocolate is melted, gradually stir in whipping cream; stir until smooth. Remove from heat. Beat egg yolks with whisk. Gradually stir some of hot mixture over eggs. Pour egg mixture back into double boiler, stirring constantly. Add vanilla, spoon into small cups. Refrigerate. At serving time, add dollop of whipped cream.

Yield: 6 servings

GRANDMOTHERS CHOCOLATE PUDDING

1 cup sugar	2 egg yolks, beaten
¼ teaspoon salt	⅓ cup cocoa
⅓ cup flour	1 tablespoon butter
2 cups milk, divided	½ teaspoon vanilla
	Frozen topping mix, optional

Sift sugar, salt and flour into top of double boiler. Stir in ⅓ cup milk and beaten egg yolks; mix until well blended. Add remaining milk and cocoa; cook until thick, stirring constantly. When thickened, remove from heat; stir in butter and vanilla. Pour into dessert cups; chill. Serve with frozen topping or whipped cream if desired.

This may also be used as a chocolate pie filling. Pour into baked pie shell or graham cracker crust. Top with meringue and brown slightly or top with frozen topping.

CHOCOLATE SEDUCTION

2½ ounces unsweetened chocolate	1 teaspoon vanilla
¾ cup butter, divided	½ (1 pound) box Oreo cookies
1¼ cups sugar	4 tablespoons butter, melted
¼ cup half and half cream	
2 eggs	

Melt chocolate and ½ cup butter in a double boiler. Add sugar and half and half cream; stir until the sugar is dissolved. Add eggs and mix well. Add vanilla. Process or finely grind the Oreo cookies. Melt remaining 4 tablespoons of butter; mix with cookie crumbs. Press into the bottom of a spring pan. Pour chocolate mixture over the crust; Bake for 45 minutes in a 350 degree oven.

INDIAN PUDDING

4 cups milk
½ cup cornmeal
½ cup sugar
7 eggs
¼ cup brown sugar, packed
⅓ cup molasses

½ teaspoon cinnamon
½ teaspoon ginger
½ teaspoon nutmeg
pinch of salt
1 cup raisins

Heat milk in a double boiler. When it begins to simmer add cornmeal and granulated sugar. Beat eggs, brown sugar, molasses, cinnamon, ginger, nutmeg and salt together. Add to the hot milk mixture. Pour pudding into a loaf pan and then add raisins. Place loaf pan in a large pan with about one inch of hot water in it. Place in a 400 degree oven and bake for 1½ hours or until pudding is firm and lightly browned.

BUTTER PECAN MOUSSE

¾ cup pecans
1 tablespoon butter or
 margarine, melted
2 (8 ounce) packages
 cream cheese, softened

¼ cup sugar
¼ cup brown sugar,
 (firmly packed)
½ teaspoon vanilla
1 cup whipping cream

Mix pecans and butter until pieces are coated. Spread on a baking sheet and bake at 350 degrees for about 5 minutes or until nuts are toasted. Allow nuts to cool, then finely chop. Beat softened cream cheese in an electric mixer until smooth. Add sugars and vanilla; beat well. Stir in nuts. Whip cream and fold it into cheese mixture. Spoon into 4 to 6 individual serving dishes.

QUICK GEORGIA PEACH COBBLER

1 stick margarine
1 cup sugar
2 cups sliced peaches

1 cup biscuit mix
1 cup milk

Melt margarine in casserole. Mix peaches and sugar, and pour into dish. Mix milk and biscuit mix, pour on peaches. Bake at 400 degrees for 40 minutes. Other fruits may be used; apples, strawberries, blueberries. Quick and easy.

MERINGUE SHELLS

4 egg whites
1 cup sugar

1 teaspoon vanilla
¼ teaspoon cream of tartar

Beat egg whites until stiff. Sift sugar and cream of tartar together. Gradually add to egg whites, beating until mixture is stiff and holds shape; add vanilla. Line cookie sheet with waxed paper. Drop and shape whites with spoon. Bake in a preheated 250 degree oven for 1¼ to 1½ hours. Turn off heat and allow to cool in oven.

ICE CREAM TRUFFLES

16 ounces dark
   unsweetened chocolate
1 cup butter
½ cup heavy cream

2 ounces Kahlua
4 cups coffee ice cream
2 cups roasted nuts,
   chopped

Melt chocolate and butter in a double boiler; stir to mix. Add cream and Kahlua. Just before it boils remove from heat. Scoop small round balls of ice cream. Dip in chocolate sauce and roll in chopped nuts. Place on waxed paper lined pan and place in freezer. Freeze at least 1 hour before serving.

APPLE PIE

½ cup sugar
¼ cup brown sugar
2 tablespoons flour
¼ teaspoon salt
½ teaspoon cinnamon

¼ teaspoon nutmeg
2 tablespoons butter
Apples to fill shell or
1 can of pie sliced apples
Dough for 2 crusts

Combine and mix sugars, flour, salt, cinnamon and nutmeg. Place sliced apples in unbaked shell, pour dry mixture over apples. Place pats of butter on top and cover with top layer of dough. Make several slits in dough. Bake at 350 degrees for 30 to 40 minutes.

EGG CUSTARD PIE
Easy and delicious

1 pastry shell
3 eggs
2 cups milk

½ teaspoon vanilla
½ cup sugar
Pinch of salt

Bake pastry shell at 400 degrees for 5 minutes. Remove from oven; cool. Combine eggs, sugar and salt. Beat until blended. Gradually stir in milk. Then add vanilla; mix well. Pour filling into pastry shell. Bake at 400 degrees for 15 minutes, reduce heat to 325 degrees and bake an additional 35 minutes or until knife inserted in center comes out clean.

SOUTHERN PECAN PIE

3 eggs, beaten
¾ cup sugar
¾ cup light corn syrup
1 teaspoon vanilla

1 cup chopped pecans
3 tablespoons butter, melted
1 (9 inch) pie shell

Mix slightly beaten eggs, sugar, syrup and vanilla. Pour into pie shell. Sprinkle nuts on top and pat down. Pour melted butter over nuts. Bake at 325 degrees for 1 hour or until mixture is set.

PECAN CHIFFON PIE

4 eggs, separated
¼ teaspoon salt
1 cup sugar, divided
1 cup milk
1 envelope plain gelatin
¼ cup cold water

1 teaspoon vanilla
1 cup chopped pecans, toasted
1 (9 inch) pie shell, baked
1 cup cream, whipped and sweetened

Beat egg yolks and place in sauce pan with salt and ½ cup sugar. In separate sauce pan heat milk and pour over egg mixture. Cook over low heat; bring to a boil and cook until thickens. Remove from heat. Dissolve gelatin in water and add at once to hot mixture. Add vanilla and set custard aside to cool completely. Beat egg whites until stiff, adding remaining ½ cup sugar. Fold into cooled custard. Gradually fold in nuts. Spoon into baked pie shell and refrigerate. After pie is firm top with sweetened whipped cream. Spread on top of pie - refrigerate until serving.

CHOCOLATE PECAN PIE

½ cup butter, melted
1 cup sugar
1 cup light corn syrup
4 eggs, beaten
1 (6-ounce) bag chocolate
   morsels

1 cup chopped pecans
1 unbaked (9 inch) pie shell
Whipped cream or frozen
   topping

Combine all ingredients except whipped cream. Mix well and pour into pie shell. Bake at 350 degrees for 40 to 45 minutes or until firm. Serve warm with whipped cream.

SWEET POTATO PIE

1¼ cups sugar
½ teaspoon cinnamon
½ teaspoon nutmeg
½ teaspoon salt
2 eggs beaten
1 (12 ounce) can evaporated
   milk

1 teaspoon vanilla
2 cups mashed cooked sweet
   potatoes
1 unbaked 9 inch pie crust

Topping
¼ cup butter or margarine
½ cup chopped pecans

½ cup brown sugar
¼ cup flour

Combine sugar, cinnamon, nutmeg and salt; stir into beaten eggs; mixing well. Add milk and vanilla. Stir mixture into mashed potatoes; beat until smooth. Pour into pie crust. Bake at 425 degrees for 15 minutes. Reduce heat to 350 degrees and bake 30 minutes. While pie is baking prepare topping. Melt margarine, add flour, sugar and nuts; mix thoroughly. Sprinkle topping crumbs on pie; return to oven and bake for 10 to 15 minutes more.

PEANUT BUTTER PIE

1 (8 ounce) package cream
  cheese
¾ cup powdered sugar
¾ cup chunky peanut butter
6 tablespoons milk

½ teaspoon vanilla
1 (9 ounce) carton frozen
  whipped topping
1 graham cracker pie crust

Combine cream cheese, powdered sugar, peanut butter and milk. Beat at medium speed until well blended, 3 to 4 minutes. Add vanilla. Fold in topping mix. Spoon into graham cracker crust. For a festive look you can sprinkle peanuts or grated chocolate on top with a few dollops of topping. Refrigerate pie at least 4 hours before serving.

COCONUT CHIFFON PIE

4 eggs, separated
¼ teaspoon salt
1 cup sugar, divided
1½ cups milk
1 envelope plain gelatin

1 teaspoon vanilla
6 ounces frozen coconut
1 baked pie shell
Whipped cream - topping

Beat egg yolks. Combine yolks, salt, ½ cup sugar, milk and gelatin in top of double boiler. Cook until begins to thicken. Cool until mushy; add vanilla and coconut. Beat egg whites with remaining ½ cup sugar; fold in pie. Pour into cool pie shell. Top with whipped cream.

DOUBLE LAYER PUMPKIN PIE

4 ounces cream cheese
1 tablespoon milk
1 tablespoon sugar
1½ cups frozen topping, thawed
1 graham cracker crust
1 cup milk

2 (4 ounce) packages instant vanilla pudding mix
16 ounce can pumpkin
1 teaspoon cinnamon
½ teaspoon ginger
¼ teaspoon ground cloves

Mix softened cream cheese, milk and sugar in a large bowl; whisk until smooth. Gently stir in frozen topping. Spread on bottom of pie crust. Pour 1 cup milk into bowl, add instant pudding. Beat with whisk until well blended, about 1 to 2 minutes. This will be thick. Stir in pumpkin, cinnamon, ginger and cloves; mix well. Spread over cheese layer. Refrigerate at least 3 hours. Garnish with additional frozen topping.

HERSHEY BAR PIE

Super, delicious and easy

1 graham cracker pie shell
6 Hershey bars with almonds (1.35 ounce size)
18 to 24 marshmallows

½ cup milk
½ (9 ounce) tub whipped frozen topping

Place milk, candy bars, and marshmallows in top of double boiler and melt. When melted set out of water and cool completely. Fold frozen topping into the chocolate. Pour into pie crust and chill in refrigerator for at least 3 hours or until ready to serve.

VELVET ALMOND FUDGE PIE

1 cup slivered almonds
1 (4 ounce) package
chocolate fudge pudding
and pie filling
¾ cup light corn syrup
¾ cup evaporated milk

1 egg, slightly beaten
½ cup chocolate chips,
melted
1 graham cracker pie crust
whipped cream

Chop almonds and toast at 350 degrees for 3 to 5 minutes. Set aside. Blend together until smooth, pie filling mix, corn syrup, milk, egg and melted chips. Add almonds and pour into pie crust. Bake at 375 degrees about 45 minutes, or until top is firm and begins to crack. Cool at least 4 hours. Garnish with whipped cream.

STRAWBERRY PIE

1 cup sugar
2 tablespoons white
corn syrup
3 tablespoons cornstarch
1 cup water

3 tablespoons strawberry
flavored gelatin
3 to 4 cups strawberries
1 9-inch pie shell, baked

Combine sugar, syrup, cornstarch, and water. Boil stirring constantly until mixture becomes clear and thickens. Remove from heat; add strawberry gelatin. Mix well and set aside to cool slightly. Wash and hull strawberries cutting large berries in half. Arrange berries in cooled pie shell, either flat in layers or standing pointed end up. Pour cooled filling over berries; chill several hours before serving. Serve with whipped cream or frozen topping.

KEY LIME PIE

1 graham cracker pie shell
1 (15 ounce) can condensed
   milk
1 (9 ounce) carton non-dairy
   frozen topping

1 (6 ounce) can frozen
   limeade
Green food coloring

Mix condensed milk and softened non-dairy frozen topping mix. Add thawed frozen limeade. Add one or two drops of coloring. Stir together until smooth. Pour into pie shell. Chill several hours before serving. Doubled recipe makes 3 pies.

BLACK BOTTOM ICE CREAM PIE

2 tablespoons butter
1 (6 ounce) package semi
   sweet chocolate chips

2½ cups crisp rice cereal
coffee ice cream

Melt butter and chocolate morsels in a double boiler. Add rice cereal; mix. Do not crush cereal. Pat mixture into 9 inch pie pan using fingers. (It is messy). Fill with coffee ice cream. Decorate top of pie with grated chocolate or chips. Place in freezer. Remove from freezer a little before serving.

Be sure and cut before serving time. It is best to remove from freezer a little before serving to soften slightly.

VEGETABLES
AND
SIDE DISHES

ASPARAGUS DELIGHT

3 tablespoons margarine
3 tablespoons flour
1½ cups milk
¾ cup shredded cheddar
  cheese
2 (10 ounce) packages frozen
  cut asparagus or 2 (10½
  ounce) cans

1 cup English Peas
2 eggs, hard boiled, sliced
1 (2 ounce) jar sliced
  pimiento, drained
1 cup bread crumbs
2 tablespoons margarine
  melted

Melt 3 tablespoons margarine in a sauce pan over low heat; blend in flour, stirring until smooth. Gradually stir in milk; cook until smooth and thickened, stirring constantly. Add cheese; stir until melted. Set aside. Drain liquid from canned peas and asparagus. If using frozen, cook until tender. Make sure all stalks are cut into bite size pieces. Place half of asparagus in a greased 2 quart casserole. Add half of peas, eggs, pimiento and cream sauce. Repeat layers. Toss bread crumbs and melted margarine; sprinkle on top of casserole. Bake uncovered in a 350 degree oven for 30 minutes or until top is browned.

Serves 6 to 8

BAKED BEANS

2 (28 ounce) cans
  pork and beans
½ cup catsup
1 cup brown sugar
  (firmly packed)

1 large onion, chopped
  or sliced
5 or 6 slices bacon

Combine all ingredients, except bacon, in a lightly greased large casserole or baking pan. Lay strips of bacon across top. Bake covered at 350 degrees for 30 minutes. Remove foil cover and bake an additional 30 minutes or until liquid has cooked down.

BROCCOLI CASSEROLE

2 (10 ounce) packages frozen chopped broccoli
1 (10¾ ounce) can cream of mushroom soup
1 cup grated sharp cheese
¼ cup mayonnaise
1 onion, finely chopped
3 eggs
breadcrumbs
3-4 tablespoons margarine

Cook broccoli according to package directions. Drain well. Combine soup, cheese, mayonnaise, onion and eggs; add to broccoli. Pour into a greased 2-quart casserole. Sprinkle bread crumbs on top. Drizzle melted margarine over crumbs. Bake at 350 degrees for 30 minutes or until casserole is bubbly and crumbs are lightly browned.

ORANGE GLAZED CARROTS

1½ pounds baby carrots scraped
½ teaspoon salt
1 tablespoon butter
2 tablespoons brown sugar
1½ teaspoons cornstarch
¼ teaspoon mace
¼ teaspoon white pepper
¾ cup orange juice
½ cup raisins

Place carrots in 2 inches of boiling salted water. Reduce heat and simmer until tender; drain. In a small sauce pan melt butter; stir in sugar, cornstarch, mace and pepper. Stir while cooking about 1 minute over medium heat. Gradually add orange juice stirring constantly. Add raisins and continue cooking until mixture thickens. Pour sauce over carrots and serve.

CARROT SOUFFLÉ

2 pounds fresh carrots　　1 medium onion, grated
½ cup butter　　　　　　　3 eggs, separated

Boil carrots in salted water until tender; drain and mash well.
Add butter, grated onion and egg yolks. Beat egg whites until
stiff; fold into carrots. Put into a soufflé dish. Bake at 350
degrees for 30 minutes.

Serves 8

CAULIFLOWER SUPREME

1 medium head cauliflower　　1 (6 ounce) can sliced
salt　　　　　　　　　　　　　　mushrooms, drained
¼ cup diced green pepper　　6 to 8 slices pimiento cheese
¼ cup margarine　　　　　　　(or cheddar)
¼ cup flour　　　　　　　　　paprika
2 cups milk

Separate cauliflower into medium size pieces. Place in boil-
i　salted water. Cover and cook 10 to 15 minutes, until
tender; drain. Saute green pepper in margarine until
er; stir in flour. Gradually add milk, stirring constantly;
k until thickens. Add ½ teaspoon salt and mushrooms.
Place ½ of the cauliflower in a 1½ quart casserole. Add ½
the cheese then ½ the sauce. Repeat layers. Sprinkle top
with paprika. Place in a 350 degree oven for about 15 minutes or until lightly browned.

Serves 6 to 8

CORN CASSEROLE

1 (16 ounce) can cream corn
3 tablespoons flour
1 cup milk, warmed
3 tablespoons margarine

1 tablespoon sugar
½ teaspoon salt
Pepper to taste
2 eggs, beaten

Slightly warm corn in a sauce pan. Add flour, margarine, milk, sugar, salt and pepper. Add eggs last. Place in greased casserole. Bake 35 minutes at 350 degrees.

EGGPLANT PARMESAN

1 large eggplant
2 eggs, slightly beaten
1 cup flour or bread crumbs
½ teaspoon garlic powder
oil for frying

1 (10 ounce) package
   Mozzarella cheese slices
16 ounces spaghetti sauce
1 cup Parmesan cheese

Cut unpeeled eggplant into ¼ inch slices. Mix garlic powder into flour or crumbs. Dip each slice into egg and then into dry mixture. Fry slices in oil for 2 to 3 minutes on each side. Remove from pan and drain on paper towels. Place half of eggplant in a greased 2 quart casserole. Cover with half of spaghetti sauce, half of Mozzarella and Parmesan cheeses. Repeat layers. Bake at 350 degrees for 30 to 40 minutes.

BAKED GRITS & CHEESE

6 cups water
½ teaspoon salt
1½ cups grits
½ cup margarine

½ cup milk
½ pound (2 cups) sharp
   cheddar cheese
3 eggs, beaten

Bring water to a boil, add salt. Slowly stir in grits, reduce heat, cover and cook until done (about 20 minutes). Remove from heat' stir in margarine, milk and cheese. Mix some of hot grits in beaten eggs then stir mixture back into hot grits. Pour into a greased 3 quart baking dish. Bake for 1 hour at 350 degrees.
For fluffier soufflé, separate eggs, add beaten yolks first, then fold in stiffly beaten whites - Light and Fluffy.

MUSHROOM CASSEROLE

1 pound mushrooms
margarine or butter
8 slices white bread
1 cup finely chopped onion
½ cup chopped celery
½ cup chopped bell pepper
½ teaspoon salt

½ cup mayonnaise
2 eggs, slightly beaten
1½ cups milk
1 (10½ ounce) can cream
   of mushroom soup
½ cup or more grated
   cheese

Rinse, pat dry and slice mushrooms. Butter bread and cut into 1 inch squares. Melt 4 tablespoons of margarine in a large skillet. Saute' mushrooms, onions, celery and bell pepper until just tender. Remove from heat, add salt and stir in mayonnaise; mix well. Place half of the bread in a lightly greased 13x9x2 inch baking dish. Spoon mushroom mixture evenly over bread. Place remaining buttered bread pieces on top of mushroom mixture. Combine eggs and milk; beat. Pour over bread and mixture in baking dish. Cover and refrigerate overnight. Before baking pour mushroom soup over mixture in baking dish. Bake at 325 degrees for 50 minutes. Sprinkle grated cheese on top; return to oven for 10 minutes.

STUFFED GEORGIA SWEET VIDALIA ONIONS

4 large sweet onions
1 cup frozen English peas,
  thawed
⅔ cup sliced fresh
  mushrooms
⅛ teaspoon dried thyme

Dash of pepper
2 tablespoons margarine
¼ cup boiling water
½ teaspoon chicken
  bouillon granules

Cut slice from top of each onion. Scoop out center, leaving ½ to ¼ inch shell. Place onions in lightly greased baking dish. Combine peas, mushrooms, thyme and pepper; spoon into onions and place margarine on top. Dissolve bouillon in boiling water; pour over stuffed onions. Cover tightly with plastic wrap, folding back a small corner to allow steam to escape. Microwave on high 4 minutes. Turn dish a half turn and cook on high 4 to 5 minutes. Let stand 3 minutes.

VIDALIA ONION CASSEROLE
Delicious yet so simple

5 to 6 large onions, sliced
1 stick margarine

⅔ cup Parmesan cheese
½ cup cracker crumbs

Peel and slice onions into thin rings, then cut rings in half. Saute onions in margarine, a couple at a time until tender and opaque, but not browned. Place half of onions in a 2 quart casserole. Cover onions with half of Parmesan cheese, then half of cracker crumbs. Repeat with remaining onions, Parmesan and crumbs. Bake at 325 degrees for 30 minutes or until golden brown.

Yields 6 to 8 servings

FRIED ONION RINGS

3 or 4 medium onions
2 eggs, slightly beaten
1 teaspoon vegetable oil
⅔ cup milk

1 cup flour
1 teaspoon salt
frying oil

Cut onions in thin slices. Beat eggs, teaspoon oil and milk together. Stir flour and salt together until well mixed. Gradually add liquid mixture to flour; beat until smooth. Heat oil to 375 degrees in a deep skillet. Dip onion rings in batter. Fry in hot oil until golden on both sides.

POTATO CASSEROLE

6 medium potatoes
2 cups shredded cheddar
  cheese
¼ cup butter or margarine
1½ cup sour cream

½ cup green onions
½ to 1 teaspoon salt
¼ teaspoon white pepper
2 tablespoons margarine
  or butter

Cook potatoes in skins; cool. Peel and coarsely shred. Combine cheese and ¼ cup butter in a sauce pan over low heat; stir until melted. Remove from heat and blend in sour cream, onions, salt and pepper. Fold in potatoes. Turn into a greased 2 quart casserole. Dot with remaining 2 tablespoons butter or margarine.

SCALLOPED POTATOES I
With or Without Cheese

6 medium potatoes
4 tablespoons butter or
   margarine
4 tablespoons flour
2 cups milk
1 teaspoon salt

½ teaspoon pepper
2 cups shredded cheddar
   cheese, optional
1 medium onion, sliced

Wash and peel potatoes; cut into ⅛ inch slices. Place in cold water until ready to use. Melt butter or margarine in sauce pan over low heat. Stir in flour, salt and pepper. Cook and stir for 1 minute until smooth. Gradually add milk, stirring constantly until slightly thickened and bubbly. Arrange half the potato slices in a 12x8 inch greased baking dish. Top with half the onions, half the sauce and half the cheese. Repeat the layers of potatoes, onions and sauce, holding cheese for later. Cover dish with foil and bake for 50 minutes or until potatoes are tender. Sprinkle with remaining cup of cheese. Return to oven and bake an additional 5 minutes.

SCALLOPED POTATOES II

5 cups cooked, sliced
   potatoes
2 cups cottage cheese
1 cup sour cream

¼ cup chopped onion
2 teaspoons salt
½ cup cheese, shredded

Mix cottage cheese, sour cream, onion and salt. Carefully fold into potatoes. Place in a 1½ quart casserole and top with cheese. Bake 40 minutes at 350 degrees.

Yield: 8 servings

141

CAROLINA RED RICE

¼ po... acon
1 medium onion, chopped
2 cups long grain rice
1 (14 ounce) can diced
   tomatoes

2 (10½ ounce) can chicken
   broth
Tabasco sauce
salt and pepper
water

Fry bacon; remove from pan and crumble. Saute onions in bacon drippings until tender but not browned. Pour off excess grease. Stir in rice; cook slightly, stirring constantly until all the rice is coated. Add tomatoes and chicken broth. Add a few drops of Tabasco according to desired spiciness; salt and pepper to taste. Cover and cook over low heat 35 to 45 minutes. Cook until rice is tender. Check and stir every 10 to 15 minutes to prevent sticking and to make sure it is not cooking all the liquid out. Add water if necessary.

8 servings

FRIED GREEN TOMATOES

4 large green tomatoes
salt and pepper
1 cup cornmeal

vegetable oil or bacon
   drippings

Cut tomatoes into ¼ inch slices. Sprinkle slices with salt and pepper; dredge in cornmeal. Heat oil or bacon drippings in a heavy fry pan. Add tomatoe slices and fry until golden brown, turning once.

SPINACH CASSEROLE
A real delight

3 (10 ounce) packages frozen chopped spinach
1 (8 ounce) package cream cheese
1 (3 ounce) package cream cheese
½ cup margarine, divided
5 tablespoons lemon juice, divided
¼ teaspoon pepper
½ teaspoon ground nutmeg
½ cup sour cream
white pepper to taste
1½ cups dry herb stuffing mix

Place spinach in salted boiling water. Bring to boil again and cook for 5 minutes. Drain well, squeezing water from spinach. Place 8 ounce package of cream cheese, ¼ cup margarine, lemon juice (except for 1 teaspoon), pepper, nutmeg and the drained spinach in a sauce pan. Stir over low heat until margarine and cream cheese have melted and mixture is smooth and well mixed. Set aside. In top of a double boiler, combine the 3 ounce package of cream cheese, sour cream, the remaining 1 teaspoon lemon juice and white pepper. Stir over hot water until smooth. Place ½ of the spinach mixture into a well greased 2 quart casserole dish. Spread the cream cheese mixture over top and then add remaining half of spinach. Sprinkle stuffing mix over top. Melt remaining ¼ cup margarine; drizzle over stuffing. Bake at 325 degrees for 20 to 30 minutes or until bubbly and lightly browned.

ELEGANT STUFFED TOMATOES
Pretty and delicious

4 large tomatoes
6 slices bacon, diced
¼ cup chopped onion
1 (10 ounce) package frozen chopped spinach

1 cup sour cream
½ cup shredded Mozzarella cheese
¼ teaspoon dried basil

Cut the ends from the tops of tomatoes. Scoop out pulp and invert to drain. Fry bacon, (do not cook until completely crisp). Remove bacon and drain. Add onions to bacon drippings; saute until tender and opaque. Cook spinach 3 to 4 minutes; drain well. (Actually squeeze excess water from spinach). Combine spinach, onions, bacon, sour cream, cheese and basil. Spoon mixture into tomato shells. Place filled shells in a baking dish. Cook uncovered in a 350 degree oven for 20 to 25 minutes, depending on size and thickness of tomatos. You do not want them to split.

This can also be prepared in a microwave oven. Cover with waxed paper and bake on high 4 to 6 minutes, rotating dish every 2 minutes.

SQUASH CASSEROLE I

3 pounds squash
1 large onion, chopped
1 tablespoon sugar
4 tablespoons margarine
½ cup mayonnaise

2 eggs, beaten
1 cup shredded cheddar
  cheese, divided
1 cup cracker crumbs,divided

Cook squash and onion in salted water until tender. Drain and mash then drain again. Add sugar, margarine, mayonnaise and half the cheese and cracker crumbs. Pour into a greased 2 quart casserole. Top with remaining crackers and cheese. Cover with foil and bake at 350 degrees for 20 minutes. Remove foil and cook 5 to 10 minutes.

Yields 8 servings

SQUASH CASSEROLE II

3 pounds of squash
2 medium onions, chopped
2 medium carrots, grated
1 cup sour cream
1 (10½ ounce) can cream of
  chicken soup

1 (8 ounce) package
  cornbread or herb stuffing
½ cup margarine

Cook squash, onions and carrots in salted water until tender; drain and mash. Add sour cream and soup. Melt margarine and mix with package stuffing. Place a thin layer of stuffing mix in a greased 9x13 casserole dish. Add a layer of half the squash, a layer of stuffing, the remaining squash and end with a layer of stuffing. Bake at 350 degrees for 30 minutes.

Yields 8 servings

SWEET POTATO CASSEROLE

3 cups mashed sweet
  potatoes
1 cup sugar
2 eggs
2 teaspoons vanilla
½ cup butter, melted

TOPPING:
1 cup brown sugar, packed
½ cup flour
1 cup chopped pecans
⅓ cup butter

Combine sweet potatoes, sugar, lightly beaten eggs, vanilla and butter; mix thoroughly. Pour into a buttered 1½ quart casserole. Combine all topping ingredients and mix well with a fork. Sprinkle crumbs on top of sweet potatoes. Bake at 350 degrees for 30 minutes.

SOUTHERN HOPPIN' JOHN
A must for New Years dinner -
will bring prosperity during the coming year

2 cups dried black-eyed peas
½ pound of hamhock, ham,
  or salt pork
2 medium onions, chopped
1 medium bell pepper,
  chopped

1 cup chopped celery
2 cups water
1 cup rice
1 teaspoon salt
¼ teaspoon pepper

Place dried peas in 8 cups of boiling water. Boil for 2 minutes, remove from heat, cover and soak for 1 hour; drain. Cover beans with water again and return to heat. Add ham, onions, celery and bell pepper. Cover and simmer for about 2 hours until beans are tender. Liquid should be cooked down. Add 2 cups water, rice, salt and pepper. Cover and cook on low for 20 minutes or until rice is done. Add more water if all cooks out before rice is tender.

Yield 8 to 10 servings

VEGETABLE PIE
A one dish meal

2 (9 inch) pie crust
1 cup broccoli flowerets
1 cup cauliflower
½ cup white shoepeg corn
½ cup small English peas
¼ teaspoon salt
½ cup chopped tomatoes

½ cup mushrooms
3 tablespoons margarine
3 tablespoons flour
1½ cups milk
½ cup shredded cheddar
   cheese

Melt margarine in a small sauce pan; add flour, stir and cook until smooth. Slowly add milk, stirring constantly until thickened and bubbly; add salt. Set aside. Cut broccoli and cauliflower into small pieces. Combine all the vegetables and cheese in one of the pie crust. Pour cream sauce over vegetable mixture. Add top crust, sealing edges. Cut slits in top crust for steam to escape. Bake at 350 degrees for 45 minutes to 1 hour.

SOUTHERN FRIED APPLES

2 tablespoons butter
10 apples, cored, peeled
   & sliced
½ cup granulated sugar

½ cup brown sugar,
   packed
½ teaspoon nutmeg
½ teaspoon cinnamon

Melt butter in a large skillet. Add sugars, nutmeg, and cinnamon. Add apples and stew or "fry" slowly, stirring often, until apples are tender, and light brown in color.

CORNBREAD DRESSING

1 8x8 pan of cornbread
4 slices dried toast
3 onions, chopped
6 tablespoons margarine, divided

6 stalks celery, chopped
3 eggs
1 (15 ounce) can chicken broth
salt and pepper

Make 1 pan of cornbread. Place 4 slices of bread in 300 degree oven. Turn oven off and let bread dry out. Sauté onions in 2 tablespoons of the margarine. Place chopped celery in small amount of salted water; simmer until tender. Crumble cornbread and dried toast into a large mixing bowl. Add onions and celery. Save the water from celery in case more liquid is needed. Add eggs and mix well. Add broth, the remaining 4 tablespoons of margarine, melted, and salt and pepper to taste. This should be soft and very moist. More margarine may be added and celery water. Pour into a greased 13½x8¾ casserole. Bake at 350 degrees until set and browned, 25 to 30 minutes.

MACARONI CASSEROLE

1 (8-ounce) box elbow macaroni
1 (10½ ounce) can cream of mushroom soup
½ cup mayonnaise
1 (2 ounce) jar pimiento

¼ cup chopped onions
1 pound sharp cheese, grated
3 tablespoons butter, melted
½ cup crushed Ritz crackers

Cook macaroni as directed on package. Mix soup and mayonnaise; add pimiento, onions and cheese. Add macaroni and mix well. Place in a 2 quart casserole and top with crackers. Drizzle butter over top. Bake in a 300 degree oven for 25 minutes.

Serves 12

HOT CURRIED FRUIT

1 (29 ounce) can peaches
1 (20 ounce) can pineapple chunks
1 (11 ounce) can mandarin oranges
1 (16½ ounce) can pitted Royal Ann cherries (optional)

1 (29 ounce) can pears
1 (17 ounce) can apricots
¼ cup sugar
3 tablespoons flour
3 tablespoons margarine
½ cup raisins
1 teaspoon curry powder
½ cup white wine

Drain fruit, reserving juices. Combine all the juices, stir to blend. Measure out ¾ cup. Combine sugar and flour in a saucepan; mix well. Gradually stir in the ¾ cup fruit juice; add margarine and raisins. Cook over medium heat, stirring constantly, until mixture comes to a boil. Boil 1 minute, continue to stir. Remove from heat and gradually stir in wine and curry powder. Place fruit in a 12x8x2 inch baking dish. Pour sauce over fruit. Bake uncovered at 350 degrees for 30 minutes.

Yield 8 to 10 servings

SWEET CORN CAKES

1⅓ cups flour
½ cup yellow cornmeal
2 tablespoons brown sugar
2 teaspoons baking powder
½ teaspoon salt

2 tablespoons butter
2 eggs, beaten
1½ cups milk
¾ cup cooked corn

Combine flour, meal, sugar, baking powder and salt; stir to mix well. Cut butter in until well mixed. Add milk to beaten eggs. Stir into dry ingredients; mix until batter is smooth. Fold in corn. Fry on a greased griddle or skillet over medium heat until covered with bubbles. Turn and brown on other side.

NOTES

INDEX

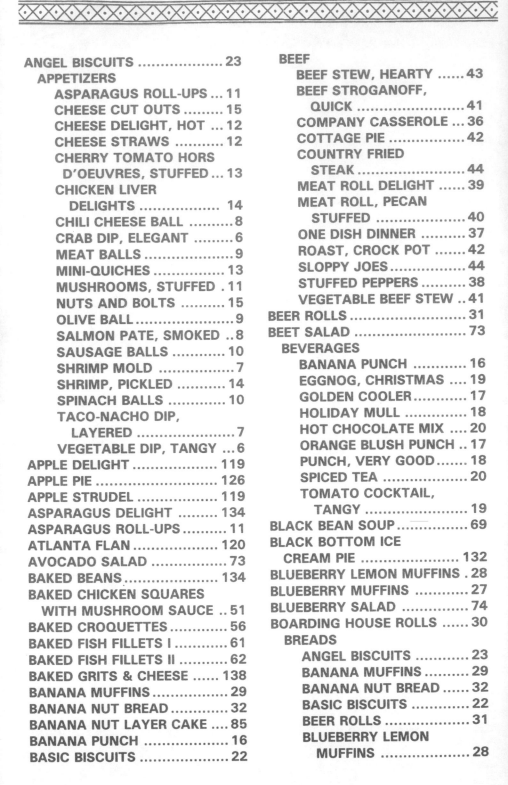

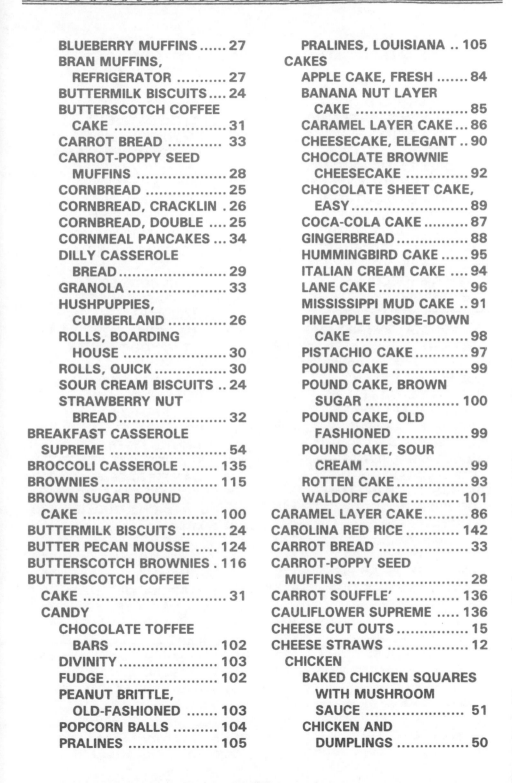

155

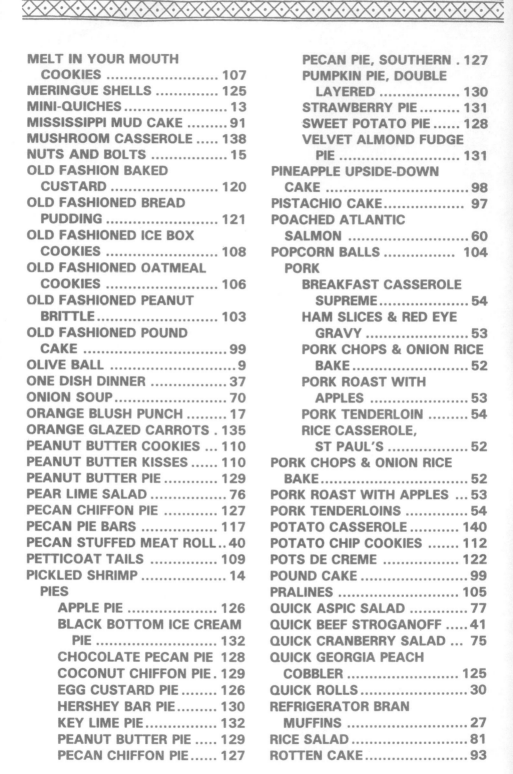

Please send _____ copies of **DELIGHTFULLY SOUTHERN** at $13.95 per book plus $2.00 shipping for 1st book and .75¢ for each additional copy. Georgia residents add 7% sales tax.

DELIGHTFULLY SOUTHERN
P.O. Box 935
Waycross, GA 31502
FAX 912-285-0349

Enclosed is my check or money order for _____

Name _____

Address _____

City _____ State _____ Zip _____

Phone (__) _____

••

Please send _____ copies of **DELIGHTFULLY SOUTHERN** at $13.95 per book plus $2.00 shipping for 1st book and .75¢ for each additional copy. Georgia residents add 7% sales tax.

DELIGHTFULLY SOUTHERN
P.O. Box 935
Waycross, GA 31502
FAX 912-285-0349

Enclosed is my check or money order for _____

Name _____

Address _____

City _____ State _____ Zip _____

Phone (__) _____